Purse
Pizzazz

Purse
Pizzazz

Marie Browning

Sterling Publishing Co., Inc.
New York

Prolific Impressions Production Staff:

Editor in Chief: Mickey Baskett
Copy Editor: Phyllis Mueller
Graphics: Lampe-Farley Communications
Styling: Lenos Key
Photography: Jerry Mucklow, John Yanyshyn
Administration: Jim Baskett

Library of Congress Cataloging-in-Publication Data

Browning, Marie.
    Purse pizzazz / Marie Browning.
        p. cm.
    Includes index.
    ISBN 1-4027-1444-0
    1. Handbags. 2. Fancy work. I. Title.
    TT667.B76 2005
    646.4'8—dc22
                                        2004019725

10 9 8 7 6 5 4 3 2 1

Published in paperback in 2006 by Sterling Publishing Co., Inc.
387 Park Avenue South, New York, N.Y. 10016
©2005 by Prolific Impressions, Inc.
Produced by Prolific Impressions, Inc.
160 South Candler St., Decatur, GA 30030
Distributed in Canada by Sterling Publishing
c/o Manda Group, 165 Dufferin St., Toronto, Ontario, Canada M6K 3H6
Distributed in the United Kingdom by GMC Distribution Services,
Castle Place, 166 High Street, Lewes, East Sussex, England, BN7 1XU
Distributed in Australia by Capricorn Link (Australia) Pty. Ltd.
P.O. Box 704, Windsor, NSW 2756 Australia

Printed in China
All rights reserved

Sterling ISBN-13: 978-1-4027-1444-3 Hardcover
        ISBN-10: 1-4027-1444-0
        ISBN-13: 978-1-4027-4065-7 Paperback
        ISBN-10: 1-4027-4065-4

For information about custom editions, special sales, premium and corporate purchases, please contact Sterling Special Sales Department at 800-805-5489 or specialsales@sterlingpub.com

Acknowledgements

I recommend supporting local craft, art supply, and hardware stores whenever possible. I thank these manufacturers for their generous contributions of quality products and support in the creation of the purse projects.

Bagworks, Fort Worth, Texas, USA, www.bagworks.com
For purse blanks, tote bags, purse handles, purse embellishments, fringe, charms, purse hardware

Blue Moon Beads, Van Nuys, California, USA, www.bluemoonbeads.com
For beads, findings, charms, pendants

Delta Technical Coatings, Inc., Whittier, California, USA, www.deltacrafts.com
For acrylic paints, adhesive fabrics

Environmental Technologies, Fields Landing, California, USA, www.eti-usa.com
For Envirotex Lite, a two-part resin coating

Fiskars Inc., Wausau, Wisconsin, USA, www.fiskars.com
For art knives, hand drill, paper trimmers, cutting mats, rotary cutter, decorative edge scissors

Hunt Corporation, Philadelphia, Pennsylvania, USA, www.hunt-corp.com
For opaque paint markers

Plaid Enterprises, Norcross, Georgia, USA, www.plaidonline.com
For decorative papers, Royal Coat® decoupage mediums, cigar box purses, FolkArt® acrylic paints

Prym-Dritz Corp., Spartanburg, South Carolina, USA, www.dritz.com
For purse handles, fabric purse blanks, purse hardware

Stone bridge Collection Inc., Pakenham, Ontario, Canada, www.stonebridgecollection.com
For wooden boxes

Walnut Hollow, Dodgeville, Wisconsin, USA, www.walnuthollow.com
For wooden boxes

About Marie Browning

Marie Browning is a consummate craft designer who has made a career of designing products, writing books and articles, and teaching and demonstrating. You may have been charmed by her creative acumen but not been aware of the woman behind it; she has designed stencils, stamps, transfers, and a variety of other award winning product lines for art and craft supply companies.

She is the author of five books on soapmaking: *Beautiful Handmade Natural Soaps* (Sterling, 1998), *Melt & Pour Soapmaking* (Sterling, 2000), *300 Handcrafted Soaps* (Sterling, 2002), *Designer Soapmaking* (Sterling 2003), and *Totally Cool Soapmaking for Kids* (Sterling, 2004). In addition to books about soapmaking, Browning has authored eight other books published by Sterling; *Handcrafted Journals, Albums, Scrapbooks & More* (1999), *Making Glorious Gifts from your Garden* (1999), *Memory Gifts* (2000), *Hand Decorating Paper* (2000), *Crafting with Vellum and Parchment* (2001), *Jazzy Jars* (2003, *Wonderful Wraps* (2003), and *Really Jazzy Jars* (2005). Her articles and designs have appeared numerous home décor and crafts magazines and in numerous project books published by Plaid Enterprises, Inc.

Marie Browning earned a Fine Arts Diploma from Camosun College and attended the University of Victoria. She is a Certified Professional Demonstrator, a design member of the Crafts and Hobby Association and a member of the Society of Craft Designers (SCD). Marie also is on the trend committee for SCD that researches and writes about upcoming trends in the arts and crafts industry. In 2004 Marie was selected by *Craftrends* trade publication as a "Top Influential Industry Designer."

She lives, gardens and crafts on Vancouver Island in Canada. She and her husband Scott have three children: Katelyn, Lena and Jonathan. Marie can be contacted at www.mariebrowning.com.

PURSE PIZZAZZ

A Brief History of the Purse

Handbags became essential when people wanted to carry something precious. While the idea of the basic bag has not changed much over time, the items inside have. Greek and Roman art shows men and women with small pouches, developed when the need arose to carry coins. The pouch, which was worn around the waist attached to a belt, was called a *byrasa* (Greek) or a *bursa* (Roman).

In the Middle Ages, the pouches were called *almonieres* or "alms bags." Traveling knights carried them and gave alms to the poor. The mistress of the castle carried a chatelaine around her waist that held her necessities such as scissors, a pincushion, and keys.

In the 15th century, women's pockets were attached to ribbons, worn under their skirts, and called "girdle pouches." When the pouches appeared on the outside of dresses, they were elaborately embroidered and adorned with jewels. These were used to show status—the richer the person, the more ornate the bag. Instead of designer logos, heraldic symbols and family crests adorned the bags, announcing the court and lineage of the owner. During this time, leather bags with drawstring fasteners were used by travelers and carried diagonally across the body.

In 1670, breeches with built-in pockets came into fashion and men dispensed with their pouches. They did still, however, continue to carry a little "purse" for money inside the pocket. The 17th century saw more variety—women carried small purses with complex shapes—but by the late 18th century, pouches for both men and women had disappeared from fashion.

In the early 19th century, women's straight-falling neo-classical dresses did not contain pockets, which would have caused unsightly bulges. Out again came the purse, then known as a "reticule," made of velvet and silk and embellished with ribbons and tassels. In a reticule one might find rouge, face powder, a fan, a scent bottle, calling cards, a card case, and smelling salts. (The word "ridicule" comes from this period, as men would poke fun at the women for carrying these bags.) Women carried a different bag for every occasion, and there was disagreement over the proper way to carry it.

The purse's most recent renaissance came around the turn of the 20th century, with the advent of the hobble skirt. Again, fashion made pockets impossible, and large handbags carried by long strings or chains became popular. The term "handbag" first emerged in the early 1900s and generally referred to hand-held luggage bags carried by men. These proved an inspiration for new bags that became popular for women and included complicated fasteners, internal compartments, and locks.

The 1920s saw higher hemlines and lighter clothing. Women, now in the workforce in larger numbers, used a handbag to carry money, keys, wallet, and identification. The purse has remained a functional and fashion item, reflecting personal style.

In the 50s and 60s, handbags had to match your shoes! The 50s also saw the rise of designer handbags by the likes of Chanel, Louis Vuitton, and Hermes, adorned with the maker's initials.

Purses today have become the second largest selling fashion accessory (after jewelry). There are purses and handbags for every mood, outfit, and occasion in a wealth of textures and materials from synthetics to natural handwoven straws.

A woman's bag today might contain a wallet for money, credit cards, and identification; a cell phone; a handheld organizer and extra batteries; a journal; tissues; sunglasses; reading glasses; a make-up bag; a brush; breath mints; a pen; a checkbook; a pager; and keys. And when a purse is not enough, we carry totes, business cases, backpacks, laptop cases, and shoulder bags. There are waterproof bags for rainy days, straw and plastic totes for the beach, bags made of glittering fabrics and decorated with rhinestones for evening, and shoulder bags for casual wear.

The Allure of the Purse

Purse, handbag, clutch, pocketbook, shoulder bag, tote, or satchel—whatever you call it, it's the one fashion accessory most women *never* leave home without. Purses are more than a container for life's portable necessities—today's bags are major fashion statements. When I started researching the subject of purses and handbags for this book, I found an explosion of innovative design. Classic leather-tone handbags look out of place in the huge array of colorful, unique handbags currently the rage.

It's been said that there are two types of people in the world: (1) women who are obsessed with handbags and (2) men. Of course, this isn't true, but for every woman who doesn't care about her purse, there's another who is crazy for fashion's most creative fashion expression. Sometimes a completely impractical bag is the most popular! Some women pay hundreds, even thousands—up to $80,000 for the Hermes Birkin bag, called the most exquisite handbag made. (Remember the *Sex in the City* episode when Samantha went to absurd lengths to acquire one?)

Cigar Box Purses

Cigar boxes are made of thin slices of mahogany or cedar that are covered with paper. They come adorned with attractive logos, company brand names, and colorful labels that are as beautiful as they are functional. In Depres-sion-era America, "tramp art" was a blue-collar craft that made beauti-ful objects from wooden ci-gar boxes. It was popular and wide-spread at a time when nearly all men smoked and knew how to whittle.

Today's cigar box purses are stunning, func-tional pieces of art, beautifully lined in suede and embel-lished with brass fittings and silk tassels. At the 2004 Academy awards, gift bas-kets for Best Supporting Ac-tor/Actress and Best Actor/Actress nomi-nees held designer Amy Schwab's ci-gar box purses.

I have included instructions for turning a cigar box into a purse, as well as many projects that use plain cigar box blanks as the base for the popular box purse.

Make a Stylish Statement

The rules are simple; don't play it safe, make a statement! A handmade purse is sure to elicit "oohs" and "ahhs" when you carry it or give it as a gift. When you're casually dressed, a handmade novelty purse can dress up your outfit and be a conver-sation starter.

The purse projects in this book cel-ebrate different personalities—they are whimsical, luxurious, elegant, casual, ro-mantic, or quirky. Allow these pages to inspire you to make your own stylish statement. Let your creativity flow and create a fashionable look that is uniquely yours.

> *"If a bag is attractive, it makes you feel good by default. It's all about proportion, shape, line, finish, fabric, balance. If all of that is pleasing it will sell. More than that it's like you've gotta have it or you'll die."*
> — Tom Ford,
> Creative Director, Gucci

Giving the Gift of a Purse

I was taught when you gave a purse as a gift you should always place some money in it for good fortune. This little pouch filled with "purse essentials" along with a gift tag is a cute way of sending good luck to the recipient. Include any special care instructions for the purse on the tag as well.

PURSE ESSENTIALS:

MARBLE – if you lose one
STRING – to keep things together
PENNY – for good luck
KISS – for love
QUARTER – to phone a friend
UMBRELLA – to shelter you in bad weather

I ENJOYED CREATING
THIS PURSE FOR YOU!

_____

Purse Essentials:

MARBLE – if you lose one
STRING – to keep things together
PENNY – for good luck
KISS – for love
QUARTER – to phone a friend
UMBRELLA – to shelter you in bad weather

I ENJOYED CREATING
THIS PURSE FOR YOU!

Marie

General Supplies

Purse Blanks

There are a wide variety of surfaces to adorn and create your own purses.

Fabric purse blanks, which come complete with handles and closures and are designed specifically for decorating, are readily available at crafts and fabric stores. These ready-to-use bags make it fun and easy to create your own customized purses. The fabric surface can be painted, appliqued, faux beaded, embellished, and accented. Some have handle loops that snap or button so changing the handle is a breeze.

Tote bags, which are in many different styles and sizes, are also easy to find. The heavy canvas surfaces are both practical and easy to decorate.

You can buy **fabric purses** at department stores—look for simple styles without outside pockets that could interfere with your design. Or sew your own—a huge assortment of purse patterns are available at fabric and quilt supply stores.

Plain **wooden boxes** or **papier mache boxes** are perfect for crafting the popular box purse. Many companies make ready-to-use "cigar box" styles, complete with all the hardware attached. Find them at crafts stores. Real **cigar boxes** also make great box purses—let the labels show or cover them and use as a base. Cigar boxes come in various thicknesses of wood and in heavy cardboard. Tobacconists usually display empty boxes for sale— I've found them for $5 or less. You can also purchase blank cigar boxes that are unfinished.

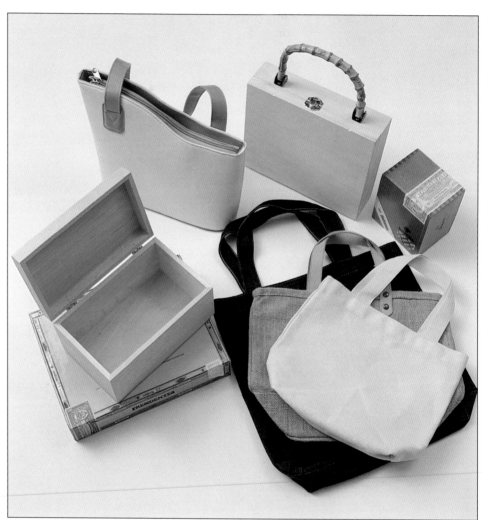

Purse Blanks

Pictured clockwise from top left: Fabric purse blank, ready-to-use cigar box, wooden cigar box (from tobacco shop), tote bags, cardboard cigar box, wooden box.

Handles & Shoulder Straps

You will need handles if you convert a box or a tote bag into a purse, or you may wish to change the handles on a purchased purse for a different look. Crafts and fabric stores are the best sources for purse handles.

Bamboo handles come in different sizes and shapes in natural, black, and burnt finishes. **Flat wooden handles**, available unfinished, are a great surface for painting, decoupage, or staining. **Plastic handles** come in a wide variety of styles and colors—clear, pearlized, simulated tortoise shell, and every color of the rainbow—and offer a very professional touch to your custom bags.

Beaded handles can be made from a kit or you can make your own for a custom look, using a strong, non-stretchy cord or 19-gauge wire. TIP: Use beads at the top of the handle that feel comfortable in your hand; keep square, rough-textured, or larger beads near the base. Wire handle frames with detachable ends can also be used for custom beaded handles.

Cabinet hardware, such as handles and drawer pulls, from home decor stores make excellent handles for wooden box purses. TIP: Make sure the opening is large enough to place your hand comfortably through it when the handle is attached to the box.

You can find **shoulder straps** in leather, chain, or cord. To make your own beaded strap, use a strong, waxed linen cord that does not stretch and is thin enough for the beads to fit on. You can also string beads on a ball-type chain for a sturdy strap. Shoulder straps can vary in length from 30" (short) to 45" (long).

Handles & Shoulder Straps

A. Bamboo handles
B. Flat wooden handles
C. Plastic handles
D. Beaded handles
E. Wire frame beading kit
F. Cabinet hardware handles
G. Beaded shoulder strap
H. Chain shoulder straps
I. Leather shoulder strap

Purse Hardware

There is a wide variety of hardware for making purses. The main components are discussed here. A variety of styles and finishes are available.

Hardware for Straps

Handle loops are placed inside handle clamps to attach handles to wooden boxes and through fabric straps on fabric purses. Many handles come with handle loops attached, but you can also buy handle loops separately. U-shaped handle loops come with a screw-on bar for attaching to the handle—just use a screwdriver.

Handle clamps secure handles to a box with handle loops. They come in a variety of sizes—make sure your handle loop is compatible with the clamp. To install, slip the handle loop through the clamp before screwing in place. Handle clamps usually come with screws; do not use nails to attach them—the nails will eventually pull out with use.

Chain hangers attach to the sides of boxes to hold shoulder straps—straps can be hooked on the hanger for use or removed when not needed. TIP: Attach the hangers in the center of the side of the box so the purse hangs comfortably balanced on your shoulder.

D-rings and rectangle rings are for attaching handles and straps to fabric purses—in a sense, they are handle loops for fabric purses. Use them when making your own fabric purses and totes and for decoration. They can be found at fabric and crafts stores.

Strap hooks come in a variety of styles, sizes, and finishes. The strap is placed through one end and a tiny screw holds it in place; the other end has a hook or clip that can be attached to a chain hanger. Most strap hooks swivel so the strap moves freely.

Closures

For box purses, purchase good quality **latches** for a secure closure. Latches are easy to find at hardware stores and come in a wide variety of styles and finishes. Choose a latch that matches the style of your purse for a coordinated, well-balanced design.

Magnetic snaps work well for closing fabric purses. They are easy to install. I used them on tote bags that I converted to purses. **Heavy duty snaps** were used to create handle loops on converted tote bags.

Hinges

Small box hinges, both plain and fancy, are readily found at hardware stores. Choose a finish that matches your other purse hardware.

Corners

Box corners add an extra decorative touch as well as protect the corners of a box purse. Some are flat; others cover all three sides of the corner. Depending on the style, they may be glued on or attached with small screws. You will need four corners for each box purse.

Supplies for Purse Interiors

Though most decorative work is done on the outside of the purse, don't forget to finish the inside with paint or stain or a decorative liner. Here are my favorite purse lining techniques and ideas for fun mirror accents.

Suede Paper

This soft, textured paper is available in many colors in plain and embossed designs for a beautiful, flocked finish. The back side is smooth so it's very easy to cut and adhere. For a straight-sided purse, measure each side carefully and cut, using a straight edge and a craft knife. Use the Chalk Transfer Method in the General Instructions for Decoupage to make a piece fit perfectly in an irregularly shaped box. Attach with spray adhesive or double-sided adhesive sheets.

Woven Back Animal Print

This is my favorite liner for purses, mainly because it comes in strong animal prints. The front feels like suede paper but the *continued on page 16*

Purse Hardware

A. Purse handle loops
B. Purse handle clamps
C. Latches
D. Hinges
E. Chain hanger

F. Box corners
G. D-ring
H. Rectangle ring
I. Strap hooks
J. Magnetic snap closure

continued from page 14
backing is woven. Measure the sides and bottom carefully and cut with sharp scissors. Use double-sided adhesive sheets (they come with animal print sheets) to attach.

Fabric-Covered Mat Board

A fabric-covered mat board adds a decorative element that helps reinforce and strengthen the purse—useful when you're using a cardboard box or a thin wooden cigar box.

1. Measure and cut the mat board to fit the bottom and sides of the purse's interior, taking the thickness of the mat board into account.
2. Place the pieces inside the box to make sure they fit perfectly and don't disturb the purse's opening and closing.

3. Use iron-on fusible webbing to adhere the fabric to the mat board, turning the raw edges under.
4. With craft glue, attach the box sides, then the bottom.

Adhesive-backed Fabric

Adhesive backed fabric is a new product available to easily line a purse. Simply measure and cut, then peel away the protective backing to reveal the adhesive. The fabric is very forgiving and initially repositionable. After a few days, the adhesive becomes permanent.

Decorative paper

Decorative paper can be decoupaged on the bottom of a box purse. Use the Chalk Transfer Method described in the General Instructions for Decoupage—it's especially handy for irregular purse shapes. Cut out the paper, adhere with decoupage medium, and coat with two or three coats of varnish to protect it.

Mirrors

Small round or square mirrors are easy to find at craft stores. Use strong jewelry glue to attach them to the inside lid of your purse. You can accent a square or rectangular mirror with flat decorative corner charms. You can also use a group of small mirrors to create a mirror mosaic.

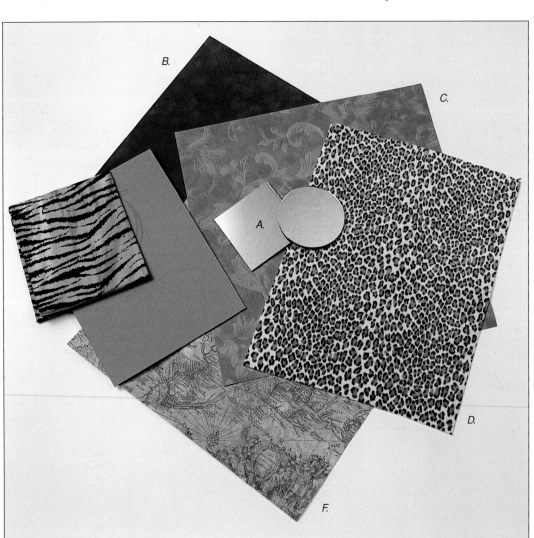

Supplies for Interiors

A. Mirrors
B. Suede paper
C. Embossed suede paper
D. Woven-back animal print
E. Fabric and mat board
F. Decorative paper

Accents

This is a small sampling of the decorative materials that you can use to embellish purses. Many crafts and sewing stores offer whole displays devoted to trims and accents for purses.

Ribbon & Trims

Ribbons are by far the easiest trims to work with and match to a project. Collect them in a variety of widths, styles, textures, and colors so you'll have a selection from which to choose. Grosgrain, satin, and wire-edge ribbons are my favorites for purse crafting.

Beautiful and inexpensive beaded trims—available in a variety of lengths and colors—are easy to find and offer great embellishment possibilities. They also can be used to make wonderful beaded fringes. Braids, rickrack, decorative fibers, and other trims—sold by the yard or by the package—are also widely available.

Look for ribbons and trims in both sewing and home decor departments.

Appliques

Appliques offer a quick, easy way to add a decorative touch to a purse. Many ready-to-use beaded appliques have adhesive backings—simply peel off and place them. Fabric, lace, and embroidered appliques can be sewn on or attached with fabric glue. Embroidered appliques also come backed with an iron-on adhesive. Look for appliques in craft and sewing stores.

Tassels

Tassels are about my favorite embellishment. Many sizes and colors are available and they are easy to find at home decor, fabric, and craft outlets. You can embellish purchased tassels with beads, some extra trim, or a ribbon rose.

It's also easy to make your own tassels from lampshade fringe or beaded fringe—here's how:

1. Cut a 10" piece of cord and 3" to 4" length of lampshade or beaded fringe.
2. Tie a knot at the end of the cord.
3. Place a line of fabric glue along the top edge of the fringe and tightly wrap it around the cord end. Let dry.
4. Further embellish with trim, beads, or a ribbon rose.

Beads, Buttons, Pendants & Rhinestones

Beads, buttons, carved pendants, and rhinestones are available in a great abundance. Glass, wood, and plastic beads can be used for beaded handles and straps; small seed bead mixes are great for the faux beaded technique. Buttons can be sewn on or the shanks can be removed with wire cutters and the buttons glued flat to the purse surface.

Both acrylic and crystal flat-back rhinestones give twinkle and sparkle to evening purses. Rhinestones also are available in prong settings.

Accents & Embellishments
A. Ribbons
B. Rick-rack
C. Upholstery braid and trim
D. Decorative fibers
E. Beaded fringe
F. Tassels
G. Feathered fringe
H. Fabric applique
I. Beaded applique
J. Carved pendants
K. Beads
L. Flat-backed faceted jewels (rhinestones)
M. Buttons

Basic Tools

Tools for Attaching Hardware

To attach purse hardware, you'll need a **small hammer** and **various small screwdrivers**, including a set used for eyeglass repair that you can use to attach the tiny screws that come with purse loops and strap hooks.

Use an **awl** for making a small hole in the wood before inserting the screw—the hole prevents the wood from splitting and makes it easier to place and start the screw so it's bites straight into the wood.

A **hand drill** with a small bit is handy for making holes in dice or other novelty items used to decorate purses. **Wire cutters** and **needlenose pliers** are essential when working with wire and jewelry findings.

Cutting & Measuring Tools

Use **sharp craft scissors** to cut ribbons and trims and to cut out paper pieces and images for decoupage. For exact, straight-line cutting, such as cutting purse linings, use a **craft knife**, a **self-healing cutting mat**, and a **metal ruler**. You'll also use the ruler to measure and mark boxes for hardware placement.

Rotary cutters are useful for cutting fabric and adhesive-backed fabric. They can cut through several layers with ease and create perfectly straight edges. They are also useful for cutting handmade paper, as a craft knife tends to rip lighter papers infused with fibers and botanicals.

Pattern Transfer Tools

Water-erase markers and **water-erase transfer paper** are great for tracing on patterns and making marks and lines on both wood and fabric purse blanks. The leftover blue lines are easily wiped away with a clean sponge and water. Find them in the fabric and painting departments of craft stores. You can also use a pencil for making marks. It is very important that you mark very lightly.

Brushes & Painting Tools

You will need a variety of good quality **artist's paint brushes** for creating painted designs:

Flat brushes - 1/2" and 1", for basecoating and painting large motifs, and #4, #6, and #10 for general painting and details

Round brushes - #1 and #4, for general painting and details

Liner brushes - #1, #0, and #00, for fine detailing

Use fine-textured **sea sponges** for basecoating and sponged finishes and dense **foam make-up sponges** for stenciling.

Other general painting supplies you'll need include **paper towels, a water basin, low-tack masking tape, and brush cleaner soap.**

Adhesives

Using the proper adhesives for different surfaces is important. The adhesive should hold up to normal use of the purse and hold your embellishments tight, even if the purse is handled roughly.

A **hot glue gun with clear glue sticks** is used when an instant, strong bond is required for trims or embellishments, but you can't re-position or remove items glued with hot glue. Use clear sticks so the glue won't be seen, and apply it in a thin stream or a small dab and adhere immediately. Hot glue is easy, quick, and waterproof, but it is not suitable for attaching some heavier items, as it does not hold up with repeated use.

Thick, tacky **white craft glue** is used for applying heavier embellishments because it creates a stronger bond than hot glue. White glue, however, can release items if a purse gets wet or in heavy humidity. Two or three coats of a good varnish will prevent this from happening. **Thin-bodied white craft glue** or **decoupage medium** is excellent for adhering paper to wooden boxes.

Specialty craft glues, such as fabric glue, jewelry glue, and wood glue, work best for specific applications (e.g., jewelry glue for attaching rhinestones to wood or fabric glue for arranging buttons on a fabric purse). Glue designed to stop cut edges of fabrics and cord ends from fraying is also valuable. These glues are white when wet but dry crystal clear.

Iron-on fusible adhesive works well for laminating fabric to mat boards and adhering transfer images to fabric purses. Because the edges are fused, there is no worry about edges unraveling or fraying, and the adhesive won't seep through fabric like glue can. The ultra-hold type is best for purse construction. Always use a pressing cloth or parchment paper to protect your iron and the transferred image when using fusible adhesive.

When gluing is not possible or will produce an inferior result, use a **needle and thread** to attach items to fabric purses. On ribbon rose purses, taking the extra time to hand sew trims and embellishments makes the purse heirloom-quality.

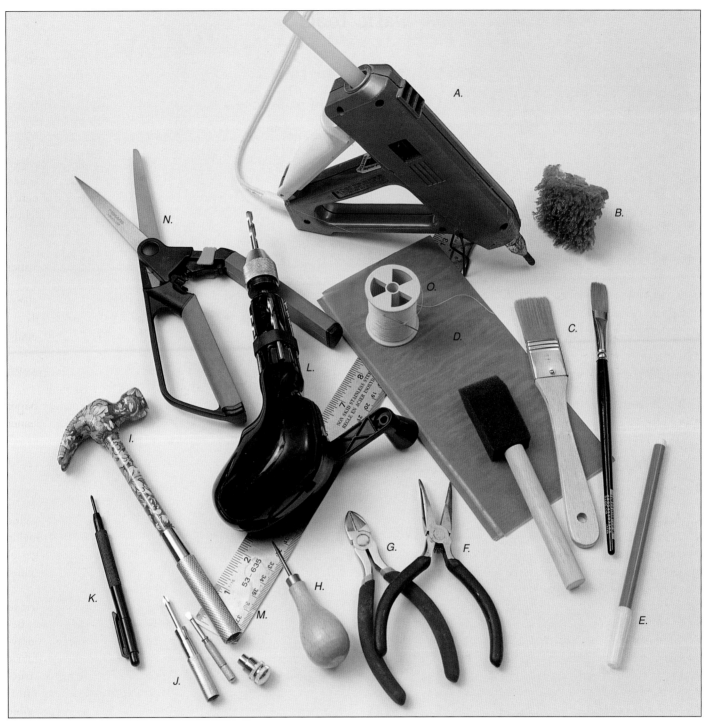

Basic Tools

A. Glue gun

B. Sea sponge

C. Brushes

D. Water-erase transfer paper

E. Water-erase marker

F. Pliers

G. Wire cutters

H. Awl

I. Hammer

J. Screwdriver set

K. Small (jeweler's) screwdriver

L. Hand drill

M. Metal ruler

N. Scissors

O. Needle and thread

General Instructions
Painting Techniques

Acrylic Craft Paints

Acrylic craft paints are suitable for painting wooden and fabric purses. They offer transparent or opaque coverage and come in a huge range of pre-mixed colors. While wet, acrylic paints clean up easily with soap and water. When dry and cured, they are durable and waterproof. TIP: **Do not** thin acrylic paints with water—instead, use blending, textile, and gel mediums manufactured for the brand of paint you are using.

Dimensional Paints

Dimensional paints (sometimes labeled "fabric paints") come in squeeze tubes. They are excellent for painting designs and accents on fabric purses. When completely dry and cured, they are remarkably strong and durable. Dimensional paints also are used for the faux beading technique.

Paint Pens

Paint pens are great for detailing and simple decoration without the fuss of paints and brushes. Paint pens come in many colors and in fine, medium, and calligraphy chisel point tips.
- Follow the manufacturer's directions for priming the pen and starting the flow of paint to the nib.
- For using a paint pen, be sure the basecoat paint on the surface has fully cured and dried.
- Paint pens can run and bleed if not protected before waterbased varnish is applied. Use a spray sealer—shake the can well and spray from 12" away with broad, even strokes to completely cover the piece with a thin protective layer of sealer. Let dry completely before varnishing.

Basecoating

In preparation for painting, remove all latches and hinges from the wooden boxes. For a smooth finish, I prefer to sand a box well after the first coat of paint is applied and dry. Two or three coats of paints are usually needed for solid coverage; be sure to let

Basecoating

each coat dry thoroughly before applying another. TIP: When covering a box side with decorative paper, paint the edges so the end result does not reveal unpainted wood.

Staining

Staining adds subtle color and allows the wood grain to show. Use **acrylic wood stains** for brown hues or mix equal amounts of acrylic paint and **glazing medium** to create your own custom tint. TIP: Test the color on the bottom of the purse.

To apply stain, use a wide brush to wipe a thin coat on one side of the box, then immediately wipe off the excess with a paper towel. To avoid dark splotches, don't leave a puddle of stain on the surface too long before wiping. When the stain has dried, sand the surface lightly to bring out the wood grain and give the box a smooth finish. Apply a second coat of stain for a darker finish.

Varnish stained wood with acrylic varnish before painting or gluing on decorative embellishments.

Stained wood

Old Wood Decorative Finish

Use this technique to create an aged, worn look on a painted purse. I prefer to work from dark to light hues when creating this decorative painted finish.

Here's How

1. Using a piece of white wax, rub the box in areas that would show natural wear, such as the edges and patches on the top and sides. The wax works as a resist, making it easier to sand off paint later.
2. Brush on a single coat of acrylic craft paint and let dry.
3. Rub more wax on the box.
4. Brush on a coat of another color paint. Let dry completely.
5. Rub more wax on the box.
6. Brush on the final paint color. Let the paint dry.
7. Sand the surface to reveal the various layers of paint.

Old wood decorative finish. I applied dark green, then medium green, then light sage green.

Sponging

You can create many delicate, fascinating patterns with `sponging. The finished surface should not look harsh or show the sponge shape. What you want is a painted finish with a colorful, interesting surface.

Here's How

1. Apply a solid basecoat. Let dry.
2. Dampen a sea sponge with water and squeeze out the excess. Pour puddles of your selected paint colors on a paper plate. Dip the sponge in one paint color and work the paint up into the sponge by tapping it on a paper towel. (You do not want too much paint on your sponge or the pattern will be too harsh.)
3. Lightly pounce the sponge on the basecoated surface to create a subtle pattern. There is no need to completely cover the surface; let a bit of the base color show through.
4. Repeat with other paint colors.

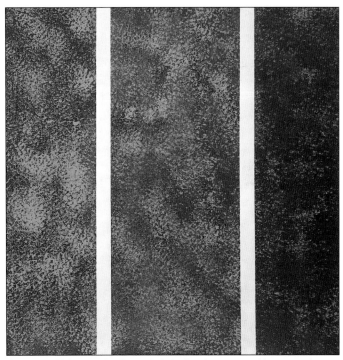

Sponging. This sample shows a dark plum basecoat with sponged layers of light coral, burgundy, and dark plum.

Transferring a Pattern

The basics are the same for transferring a pattern to a wood or fabric purse blank.

1. Use translucent **tracing paper** to trace the pattern from the book.
2. If you need to adjust the pattern size, enlarge or reduce the traced design on a photocopier.
3. Lay **transfer paper** face down on your surface and tape in place with masking tape. (I prefer blue water-erasable transfer paper—the marks can be wiped away with a damp sponge.) TIP: Always test the transfer paper before starting to make sure it leaves a mark that is easy to see but not too dark.
4. Place the pattern on top and tape in place.
5. Use a ballpoint pen to trace over the pattern lines and transfer the design to the surface. Occasionally check your progress by carefully lifting the pattern and tracing paper.

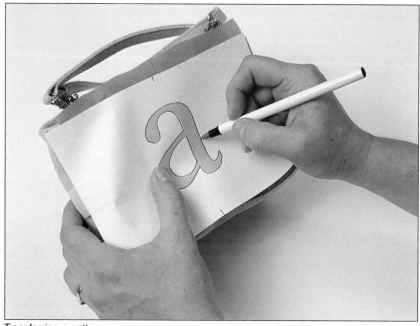

Transferring a pattern.

Making Your Own Monogram

It's easy to make your own monogram pattern for a purse using a computer—simply choose the letter and type style, then enlarge to the size required. I print out the resulting pattern in light gray to save ink.

Sample monograms. The lower case letter "a," for example, is a Times New Roman font enlarged to 400-point size.

Finishing Painted & Decoupaged Purses

Properly protecting your finished work means that it will last for years.

Painted purses need two or three coats of acrylic spray or brush-on varnish—both types come in gloss, satin, and matte finishes. **Decoupaged purses** can be finished with a protective varnish coating or a two-part pour-on resin coating.

Apply a Brush-on Varnish Finish

Use a large, soft brush to apply the varnish to the surface in slow, thin coats. The more thin coats you apply, the finer the piece will appear and the tougher the surface will be. Here's how to apply brush-on varnish:

1. Roll the varnish container to mix rather than shaking it to minimize the appearance of bubbles on your finished piece.
2. Pour a small amount of varnish in a small disposable bowl. (This prevents the large container from being contaminated from your brush.)
3. Brush on thin coats, letting each coat dry thoroughly before adding another. Let the finish cure for a few days before using.

You can also add acrylic glazes with a metallic or iridescent tone to clear varnish for a special luminous finish. Examples are the African Safari Gourd Purse, which has a gold metallic finish, and the Starlight Purse, which has a blue iridescent finish.

To care for a varnished purse, simply wipe with a damp sponge. To remove tough stains or marks, gently sand until the mark is gone with a very fine grit sandpaper. Re-varnish the piece, applying at least two coats.

Two-Part Resin Coating

A pour-on resin coating gives decoupaged purses a hard, waterproof finish with a depth and luster equal to 50 coats of varnish. I used it on some of the decoupage projects. Instructions for applying a resin coating appear on page 68.

Decoupage

Decoupage Papers

Decoupage on wooden purse boxes opens the design possibilities with the endless selections of beautiful papers that are now available. Lightweight decoupage paper or memory book paper is the best type to use. Printed napkins, natural papers, and collage papers are other possibilities. Another option is to make color photocopies of objects, such as the card and poker chip paper inside the Casino Purse.

Decoupage Medium

Use a "podge"-type decoupage medium or thin-bodied white glue to adhere paper to wooden surfaces. Decoupage finishes also are available in antique, sepia tone, or pearl finishes.

Cutting

TO CUT IMAGES: Trim away excess paper around the image you wish to cut out. Using a **craft knife** and **cutting mat**, cut out any inside areas. Then use small, sharp, pointed **scissors** (cuticle scissors or decoupage scissors) to cut out the images.

- Hold the scissors at a 45 degree angle to cut the paper with a tiny beveled edge. This edge will help the image fit snugly against the surface.
- Move the print, not the scissors as you cut.

After cutting out an image, you can decorate it further with stamping or antique the edges with an inkpad and a dense foam brush.

When cutting a piece of paper to completely cover a box side, use this Chalk Transfer Method for a more perfect fit than you get from just tracing around the box. It also works well for making paper fit perfectly inside a box or on a box with curved sides.

1. Using a piece of tailor's chalk, rub around the edge of the area that you wish to match.

2. Place the paper you will be using over the area and press around the edges with your fingers. This transfers a chalked line that you can easily see.
3. Cut the paper piece to size.

Gluing

Use a sponge brush or a soft bristle brush for applying the finish.

1. Cover your working surface with freezer paper to protect it.
2. *For fine, thin papers,* such as paper napkins, tissue, and fine handmade papers, brush decoupage medium on the surface, then attach the paper piece. Immediately brush decoupage medium over the paper to adhere it and smooth out any wrinkles.
3. *For medium weight paper motifs,* lightly coat the back of the image with decoupage medium. Position the image on the surface and smooth with your fingers, pushing out wrinkles and air bubbles. Allow to dry before proceeding.

TIP: For a perfectly matched image on a box seam, glue the motif over the box seam and let the decoupage medium dry completely. Then use a sharp craft knife to cut the image at the seam.

Sealing

Option 1: Apply two to three coats of decoupage medium with a foam brush. The finish appears cloudy when wet, but will dry crystal clear.

Option 2: If you are planning to coat your project with pour-on resin, use this method. Coat the decoupaged surface with thin-bodied white glue to seal.

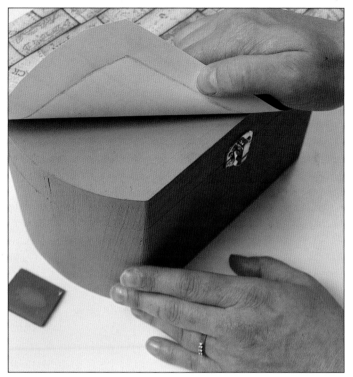

Using the Chalk Transfer Method to mark paper for a perfect fit

Applying decoupage medium to a surface before attaching thinner papers, such as paper napkins or printed tissue

Applying decoupage medium to back of cutout motif

Converting a Tote Bag to Make a Purse

Here's an easy, economical way to make a purse blank that will hold standard handles from a small tote bag. The snaps allow you to change handles easily. Small (8" x 10") fabric tote bags are widely available in natural canvas and denim as well as in black and bold primary colors.

If you like, you can add a magnetic snap closure and put a piece of heavy mat board on the inside bottom of the tote. (This gives a sturdy bottom to the finished purse. For a small tote, cut a 3" x 8" piece of mat board.)

Supplies

Small tote bag
Scissors
4 sets heavy duty snaps
Hammer and snap setting tools
Wooden board (for setting snaps)
No-fray adhesive (keeps raw, cut edges from unraveling)
Handles
Optional: Magnetic closure snap, piece of mat board, glue gun and clear glue stick

Instructions

1. Measure and cut the straps, leaving 2-1/2" from the top of the bag edge. (photo 1)
2. Add the snaps, following the package instructions. (photo 2)
3. Apply the no-fray glue to the cut ends to prevent unraveling. Let dry until clear. (photo 3)
4. Fold loops over the handle and snap in place. (photo 4)
5. *Option:* Attach a magnetic closure snap at the center of the top edge, carefully cutting the stitches and placing the snap inside the top hem. After the snap is in place, stitch or glue the opening closed.
6. *Option:* Cut a piece of mat board to fit the bottom of the bag. Secure with hot glue.

Photo 1. Measuring and cutting the straps

Photo 2. Adding the snaps

Photo 3. Applying no-fray adhesive to the cut ends

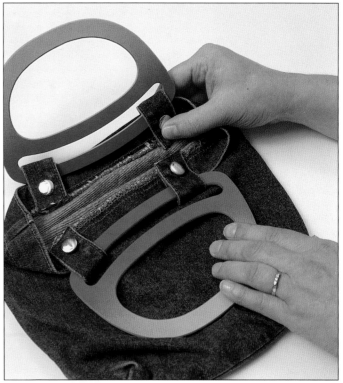

Photo 4. Attaching the handles

Beading Basics Here are some helpful hints for working with beads:

- **Use a wire needle for stringing beads.** Fold an 8" length of thin beading wire in half and twist to form a wire needle to string beads on cord, ribbon, or thread. *Option:* Purchase wire bead needles.

- **Clean the hole.** Some glass beads come with a white chalky material inside the hole that tends to prevent the bead from being threaded on a cord. If that's the case, use a bead reamer to clean out the hole. You also can use a reamer to make a hole larger, even on a glass bead.

- **Choose the right wire.** 20 or 22 gauge wire works well for flexible bead-and-wire handles and straps. For sturdy, inflexible handles that keep their shape, use heavier (e.g., 18-gauge) wire.

- **Use beading needles for sewing.** Use a #10 or #12 beading needle for sewing small beads. Beading needles have narrower eyes than ordinary sewing needles. The higher the needle number, the smaller the diameter.

Cigar Box Purses

Unlike ready-to-use cigar box blanks or plain wooden cigar boxes, these purses are made from the actual boxes in which cigars were packaged. They are made of thin wood, with the lid and sides covered with a decorative paper. They are usually covered with labels and have branded labels on the exposed wooden parts. Your local tobacconist will have a selection of empty cigar boxes for sale.

You can decorate these boxes with painting or decoupage, or use them as they are to create a unique purse. Converting an authentic cigar box into a purse is simple.

Basic Supplies for Cigar Box Purses

Wooden cigar box

Handle

Handle clamps with small screws

Latch (Make sure the latch matches the box construction—some latches won't work on the thin lids.)

Optional: Chain hangers and shoulder strap, decorative corners (Use the flat type to avoid interference with closing the purse.)

Varnish and brush

Craft glue

Hair dryer

Embellishments - Additional stamps or labels such as old postage stamps, decorative stickers, or cigar labels; tassel

Liner - animal print material or adhesive-backed fabric

Basic Instructions for Cigar Box Purses

1. Remove unwanted labels or price tags from the box. TIP: If they prove stubborn and the cigar box paper starts to rip, heat the labels with a hair dryer to soften the glue. If you rip the covering paper on the box, use the extra labels and stamps as camouflage.

2. Glue down edges of any labels that are lifting up. (These labels usually are over the box seam.)

3. Add more labels to the box to hide flaws or for additional decoration.

4. Brush the entire outside of the cigar box with two to three coats of varnish.

5. Attach the handle and latch to the box. NOTE: The front of the box will be upside down on the finished purse.

6. *Option:* Add box corners to the lid.

7. *Option:* Reinforce the box hinge, if needed, by cutting a 1/2" wide strip of matching paper and gluing it inside the box over the hinge. Make sure the reinforcement does not interfere with opening and closing the lid. TIP: Strips of adhesive-backed fabric work exceptionally well for this.

8. *Option:* Finish the inside of the box by lining the bottom and bottom sides. (I don't usually varnish or cover the insides of box lids—they usually are adorned with nice images. Leaving them unvarnished retains the aroma of the cigars.)

9. Loop tassel cords around the handle.

Faux Beaded Purses

This technique is easy and effective on both wooden and fabric purses. The tiny glass marbles make the designs appear to have been meticulously sewn rather than sprinkled on wet paint. They look especially nice in candlelight.

Basic Supplies

Dimensional paints in a variety of colors (they come in applicator bottles)

1mm glass mini marbles or tiny clear seed beads (You can also use a blend of different shaped and colored beads for nice effects.)

Basic Instructions for Faux Beading

1. Transfer the pattern to the surface using water-erase transfer paper or a water-erase marker.
2. Working one area at a time, outline, then fill in the design with dimensional paint. (photo 1)
3. Sprinkle the paint with clear glass marbles or a bead mix. (photo 2) TIP: Work over a box lid to collect excess beads. You can gently shake off excess beads into the box lid and re-use them.
4. Continue adding more paint and beads until the design is complete. Let the purse lie flat and let dry completely for 12 hours before using.

Photo 1. Applying fabric paint to a pattern—outline first, then fill in the design

Photo 2. Holding the purse over a box top or tray (to catch the beads that don't stick), sprinkle beads over the wet paint

Retro Beaded Monogram ▶
Instructions appear on page 32.

Retro Beaded Monogram
Fabric Purse
Pictured on page 31

This pink and black bag has fiber-and-bead fringe and a faux beaded initial. The simple design can, of course, be created in many other color pairings. You can make the purse a unique reflection of the recipient by adding fun novelty buttons and motifs—in this case, a telephone and French poodle.

Supplies

Base & Hardware:
Black fabric purse, 6-1/2" x 8", with magnetic closure, shoulder strap removed
Beaded handle kit - Wire form with pink, ivory, and silver beads
Option: 18" of 19-gauge wire and enough beads to cover the wire.

Decorative Materials:
Pink fiber-and-bead fringe
Dimensional paint - Pink
Pink seed bead mix
Accents - Telephone novelty button, poodle charm with hole drilled and small loop attached for hanging

Tools & Other Supplies:
Water-erase transfer paper
Computer-generated initial pattern
Fabric glue
Needle and thread

Instructions

To make a pattern for the monogram, see "Making Your Own Monogram" in the General Instructions.
1. Transfer the pattern to the front of the bag.
2. Outline and fill in the letter with pink dimensional paint.
3. Sprinkle the wet paint with the bead mix. Let dry.
4. Glue the fringe around the top of the purse.
5. Construct the handle, following kit instructions. Attach to loops inside purse. *Option:* Make a handle with wire and beads.
6. With needle and thread, make a short string of beads. Add the telephone button. Make another bead string. Add poodle. Stitch the accents to the top of the purse.

Leather Rose & Beads
Fabric Purse
Pictured at right

Beaded stripes were added to this purse. The button-on purse blank and handles can be assembled quickly. It's easy to change the handle for a different look.

Supplies

Base & Handles:
Khaki twill purse blank with button-on handle loops
Wood and wooden bead handles

Decorative Materials:
Dimensional paint - Taupe
Topaz bead mix
Leather rose with pin back

Tools & Other Supplies:
Water-erase marker

Instructions

1. Using the marker, draw guidelines for the stripes, starting in the center of the purse. Make them about 1/2" apart at the top and 3/4" apart at the bottom.
2. Paint the stripes with taupe dimensional paint.
3. Sprinkle the bead mix on the wet paint. Let dry completely.
4. Add handles
5. Pin rose to the front top of the purse.

Denim & Beaded Butterfly
Fabric Purse

This casual bag sports a frisky butterfly and beaded macrame handles. Adding glitz and glamour to denim creates this young at heart purse.

Supplies

Base & Handles:
Denim twill purse blank with button handle loops and magnetic closure
4 D-rings
Blue hemp cord
16 blue glass beads
16 silver plastic beads

Decorative Materials:
Dimensional paints - Black, light blue, purple
Tiny clear glass marbles
Blue fibers
Blue seed beads
Silver heart button
4 blue buttons

Other Supplies:
Needle and black thread
Fabric glue

Instructions

1. Transfer the butterfly pattern and guidelines for fibers.
2. Working one area at a time, apply fabric paint to butterfly design and sprinkle paint with clear glass marbles. Let dry.
3. Position fibers on guidelines and sew in place with small stitches. Add a few seed beads for additional sparkle.
4. Make beaded handles. For each handle cut two pieces of hemp cord, each 1 yard long. Loop on a D-ring. Making simple square knots, string on beads to create a handle. When the handle is 10" long, attach ends to other D-ring and knot off. Repeat to make other handle. Add a small amount of glue to cut ends to prevent raveling and secure the knot.
5. Attach handles to fabric loops on purse.
6. Glue on buttons in front of loops with fabric glue.
7. Glue silver heart button on closing tab.

Pattern for butterfly

Painting guide for butterfly

She Sells Seashells & Beads
Fabric Purse

This fun, sea-inspired purse is decorated with real shells. The tassel is adorned with beads and charms and a shell that has a small hole drilled in it.

Supplies

Base & Handles:
Natural tulip shaped canvas purse blank with original handles removed
2 bamboo handles, natural colored
4 brass purse handle loops

Decorative Materials:
Shells, a variety of small ones
Gold sea-theme charms
Dimensional paint - Lilac, crystal, pale green
Tiny glass marbles
Taupe braid trim
Taupe tassel
Beads and charms
Shell mirror (Green grosgrain ribbon, round mirror (3" diameter), scallop shell (3" diameter), small shells)

Tools & Other Supplies:
Fabric glue
Strong jewelry glue
Water-erase transfer paper
Clear gloss acrylic spray

Purse Instructions

1. Seal the shells with clear gloss spray. (This brings out the colors and adds a nice finishing touch.)
2. With fabric glue, attach the shells and the gold charms. Use a good amount of the glue to make sure the shells are firmly attached. Let dry completely.
3. With dimensional paints, add curlicues to the design. Sprinkle with tiny glass marbles. Let dry completely.
4. Glue taupe braid around the top of the purse with fabric glue.
5. Adorn the tassel with beads, charms, and the shell. Use a needle and thread to tack these pieces firmly to the top of the tassel.
6. Glue the tassel cord inside a shell. Glue the shell to the braid along the top as shown.
7. Attach the handles to the fabric loops inside the purse.

Shell Mirror Instructions

1. Glue the round mirror in the scallop shell, using jewelry glue. Add one end of an 8" piece of green grosgrain ribbon between the mirror and the shell.
2. Stitch the other end of the ribbon to the inside of the purse.
3. Glue a collection of small shells around the mirror.

Night Leopard
Evening Bag

Tiny beads make a big impression on a small black cocktail purse. It is a simple technique with smashing results. In addition to the leopard design, patterns for zebra, tiger, and jaguar prints are included.

Supplies

Purse Base:
Small black fabric purse with magnetic closure and black strap

Decorative Materials:
Dimensional paint (for leopard print) - Black, tan, ochre, brown
Tiny clear glass marbles
Black tassel
Beads for tassel

Other Supplies:
Water-erase transfer paper

Instructions

1. Remove handle and set aside.
2. Trace pattern provided and transfer design.
3. Starting on one side of the purse, apply paint, filling in an area 2" square. Sprinkle with tiny beads. Allow excess beads to drop off. Continue with paint until one side of the purse is covered. Let dry completely. Then paint and apply beads to the other side.
4. Using the photo as a guide, add beads to top of tassel and attach to handle loop.
5. Reattach handle. 👜

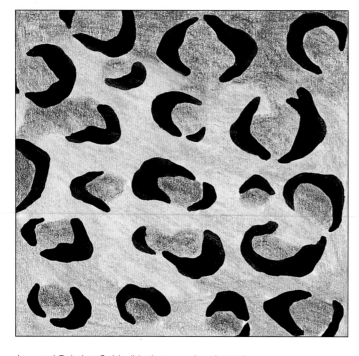

Leopard Painting Guide (black, tan, ochre, brown)

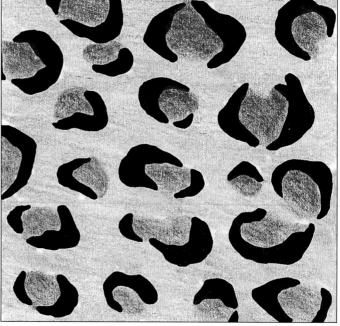

Jaguar Painting Guide (black, brown, tan)

Stamped Purses

Stamping is an easy way to add decorative motifs to surfaces. From rubber stamps that mimic the look of printing and etching to foam block printing stamps that resemble hand painting and stenciling, you'll find a range of options for creating stamped designs.

Rubber Stamps and Ink

The range of motifs available in rubber stamps is huge; whatever motif or theme you are looking for, there is a stamp available, and inks for stamping any surface you wish.

For stamping images on wooden boxes, I prefer to use a permanent inkpad because the ink will not run or smudge when coated with varnish, and I like a raised pad because it can be used with any size of stamp.

Basic Instructions for Stamping

Before stamping a wooden surface, apply a coat of acrylic varnish and let dry. If you happen to make a mistake, it can be removed immediately with the ink solvent without marring the painted surface.

1. Load the stamp evenly with the ink by lightly tapping the stamp on the inkpad.

2. Press the stamp firmly on the surface without rocking the stamp. Lift the stamp.
3. Protect the surface with two more coats of acrylic varnish.

Block Printing

The foam stamps made for block printing work well for stamping images on fabric. It is best to practice this method on a piece of fabric as mistakes are not easy, if not impossible, to remove.

Basic Instructions for Block Printing

1. Mix equal amounts acrylic craft paint and textile medium.
2. Use a flat brush to apply an even coat of the paint mix over the stamp.
3. Position the stamp on the surface. Push firmly without moving the stamp for a clear image. Lift straight up.

Fleur de Lis
Cigar Box Purse

This design uses rubber stamps to add a pattern over a stained box. Acrylic rhinestones are sparkly accents. You could choose different themed stamps and different colors for endless design possibilities.

Supplies

Purse Base:
Ready-to-use wooden cigar box purse blank, 6-1/2" x 6", with bamboo handle, hinges, and latch

Decorative Materials:
Acrylic craft paint - Light jade green
Glazing medium

Rubber stamps - Fleur de lis, castles and diamond motif stamps
Permanent ink stamp pads - Dark purple, olive green
Variety of rhinestones, different shapes - Purple, clear, green
Embossed moss green suede paper (for the inside)
Tassel with beads

Other Supplies:
Basecoating brush
Water-erase marker
Jewelry glue
Matte varnish
Cellulose sponge
Paper

Fleur de Lis Purse ▶
Instructions are on page 44.

Fleur de Lis *continued*

Instructions

1. Mix equal amounts green acrylic paint and glazing medium to make a transparent stain. Stain the inside and outside of the box with this mixture. Let dry.
2. On a piece of paper the same size as your purse front, create a trial version of your stamped design. Adjust the placement until you are pleased with the arrangement.
3. With the marker, draw guidelines for stamping the motifs. Using the stamps and the stamp pads, stamp the pattern on the front and sides of the box. Remove guideline with a damp sponge.
4. Coat the stamped pattern with two to three coats of matte varnish.
5. Glue the rhinestones on the stamped images with jewelry glue.
6. Cover the inside of the purse with suede paper.
7. Attach the tassel to one side of the handle. 👜

Primitive Art
Shoulder Bag
Pictured at right.

This purse was an experiment—I chose the colors by looking at my wardrobe and brushed on colors in simple geometric shapes, blending and mixing as I went. (Using textile medium helps the paints to adhere and blend well on fabric.) I personalized the design with hand print and accented the painting with dimensional paint scribbles and simple primitive symbols.

It turned out to be a favorite design. I've included the instructions and color combinations I used to guide you, and I challenge you to have fun, choose your own palette of colors, and create an original masterpiece.

Supplies

Purse Base:
Contour fabric shoulder bag, natural color

Decorative Materials:
Acrylic craft paints - Dark teal, maroon, terra cotta, dark brown, metallic gold, black
Acrylic textile medium
Dimensional paints - Metallic copper, terra cotta, metallic black
Rubber stamp, primitive symbol
Black permanent inkpad

Tools & Other Supplies:
Paint brushes - variety of sizes
1" sponge brush
Piece of wood shelving to fit inside purse (for a firm stamping surface)

Instructions

1. Mix each acrylic paint color with an equal amount of textile medium.
2. Using all the mixed colors except black, paint simple geometric shapes on the front of the bag, blending the colors as you go. Let dry when you are satisfied with the design.
3. With copper and terra cotta dimensional paints, add scribbles and lines to accent your painted piece. Add your signature at the bottom. Let dry completely.
4. Place the piece of wood shelving inside the purse. For the hand print, use a sponge brush to apply an even, heavy coat of black paint + textile medium to your non-painting hand. Place your hand on the purse to stamp the image. Let dry.
5. Using the rubber stamps and the black inkpad, add the primitive symbols to the composition.
6. Trace over the rubber-stamped images with black metallic dimensional paint. Use the same paint to add a simple design at the base of the strap. 👜

Stamped & Bejeweled Florals
Wooden Box Purse

Stamped designs adorned with faceted jewels decorate this stained box purse.

Supplies

Base & handle
Hinged wooden box, 4" x 8"
Black and silver clamp-on handle

Decorative Materials:
Acrylic wood stain - Honey maple
Rubber stamps - Daisy, swirl, butterfly
Permanent ink stamp pad - Black
Black paint pen, fine tip
Variety of different shaped and colored rhinestones
Black suede paper (to line the inside)

Other Supplies:
Jewelry glue
30-minute epoxy glue
Matte varnish
Basecoating brush
Water-erase marker
Clear acrylic spray
Paper
Cellulose sponge
Pliers

Instructions

1. Stain the inside and outside of the box. Let dry.
2. On a piece of paper the same size as your purse front, create a trial version of your stamped design. Adjust the placement until you are pleased with the arrangement.
3. Using the stamps and the stamp pads, stamp the design on the front and sides of the box.
4. With the marker, draw guidelines for the curled vine and butterfly flight lines. Trace over these lines with the black paint pen. Remove guidelines with a damp sponge.
5. Spray the box with clear sealer to fix the paint pen lines.
6. Apply two to three coats of matte varnish. Let dry between coats.
7. Glue the rhinestones on the stamped images with jewelry glue.
8. Attach the handle. The clamp-on style handle is generally used with a fabric purse blank. To use on a box, use pliers to bend the clamps flat and glue to the box top with 30-minute epoxy. Let set.
9. Line the inside of the box with suede paper. 👜

African Block Prints

Canvas Purse

A color wash of earth colors is painted on the bag and bold primitive symbols are block printed in black. Opulent feathered fringe and wooden animal buttons accent this African-inspired purse.

Supplies

Base & Handles:

Small natural canvas tote bag (converted to a handbag)

Two rope handles with wooden purse loops

Magnetic closure snap

4 heavy duty snaps

Antique gold D-ring

Decorative Materials:

Acrylic paints - Raw umber, burnt sienna, terra cotta, black

Acrylic textile medium

20" feather fringe

Large primitive symbol stamping blocks

3 wooden animal beads

8 gold spacer beads

6 copper beads

10" fine beading wire

Tools & Other Supplies:

Basecoating brush

1" sponge brush

Fabric glue

Instructions

Do the painting before converting the tote bag into the purse.

1. Mix each color of acrylic paint with an equal amount of textile medium. (This helps the paints to adhere and blend well on the fabric.)

2. Basecoat the outside of the bag, the inside edge, and the handles with the raw umber, burnt sienna, and terra cotta paint mixtures. Brush and blend the colors together for a mottled look. Let dry.

3. Follow the instructions for "Converting a Tote Bag to Make a Purse" in the *General Instructions* section.

4. Load the stamping blocks with a thick, even coat of the black paint mixture. Stamp on the front of the bag. Let dry.

5. Using dimensional paint as a glue, adhere the feather fringe to the top edge of the bag.

6 Use fine beading wire to thread beads and wooden animal beads together to form the accent. Attach the wire ends to the D-ring.

7. Attach the D-ring to the purse handle.

Painted Purses

Painted designs can take a variety of guises and be a background for further embellishments—painting is a terrific way to showcase your artistic vision. See the General Information section for information on painting supplies and techniques.

Martini Girl

Cigar Box Purse

Pattern appears on page 52.

This whimsical design is decorated with faux beading, painting, and stenciling over a stained base.

Supplies

Purse Base:
Ready-to-use cigar box purse with hinges, latch, and handles, 7-1/2" x 9"
4 brass corners

Decorative Materials:
Wood stain - Walnut
Acrylic craft paints - Dark brown, light brown, black, white, green, yellow
Alphabet stencil
Black paint pen with fine tip
Iridescent blue glaze
Clear dimensional paint
Tiny glass marbles
Taupe tassel
Red rhinestones
Dark red suede paper (for lining the purse)
Mirror mosaic - five 1" square mirrors, five 1/2" square mirrors, four 1/2" square green rhinestones, one red round rhinestone, seven clear round rhinestones

Tools & Other Supplies:
Water-erase transfer paper and marker
Paint brushes - basecoating and detail
Jewelry glue
Gloss varnish

Instructions

1. Stain the inside and outside of the box with walnut stain. Let dry.
2. Using the alphabet stencil with brown and black paints, stencil the words. I used "Martini," "Vermouth," "Olive," and "Gin" and repeated them with both the black and brown paints. Use the marker to make guidelines to keep the lettering straight. It's okay if the words run together or spill over the edge of the box—they're meant to be an interesting background. Let dry.
3. Transfer the glass and olive pattern to the box
4. Paint the design, using the pattern as a guide for applying color.
5. Brush a coat of iridescent blue glaze over the martini glass design. Let dry completely.
6. Use the black paint pen to add details and outline design.
7. With the clear dimensional paint, fill in the glass as indicated on the pattern. Sprinkle with tiny marbles. Let dry.
8. Glue red rhinestones in the olives.
9. Line the inside bottom of the purse with red suede paper.
10. Use mirror pieces and red, green, and clear rhinestones to create a mosaic in the shape of a martini glass inside the lid (complete with a rhinestone olive!)
11. Attach the brass corners and the tassel.

Paint olives green

White

Yellow

Green

Apply dimensional paint here

White

Martini Girl Purse pattern
Actual size

Checkmate Purse pattern
Actual size

Instructions on page 54

Checkmate
Cigar Box Purse
Pattern appears on page 53.

This box purse is painted with a bold design that offers a sophisticated finished piece. The chess piece is an undemanding design for a beginner to paint.

Supplies

Purse Base:
Ready-to-use wooden cigar box purse, 7-1/2" x 9", with hinges, latch, and handles
4 brass corners

Decorative Materials:
Acrylic wood stain - Cherry
Acrylic craft paints - Black, metallic gold, dark brown, burnt sienna, white
12 small clear acrylic rhinestones
Black tassel
Black plastic chess piece
Black suede paper (for lining)

Tools & Other Supplies:
Jewelry glue
Low-tack masking tape, 1-1/2" wide
Paint brushes - basecoating, detail brushes
Permanent black marker, fine tip
Gloss varnish
Water-erase transfer paper
Drill and drill bit

Instructions

1. Stain the inside and outside of the box with cherry stain. Let dry.
2. With the masking tape, tape off the checkerboard design on the front of the box.
3. Paint the front of the box with black. When dry, remove the tape to reveal the checked design.
4. Transfer the chess piece outline to the front of the box.
5. Paint the chess piece solidly with metallic gold. (You'll need two or three coats for complete coverage.)
6. Re-position the pattern and, using transfer paper, trace over the details.
7. Following the pattern, shade and highlight the design. Use a scrubbing motion with very little paint on your brush. Let dry.
8. Add details with a black marker.
9. Glue the rhinestones in the corners of the checkerboard.
10. Attach the four brass corners to the box.
11. Line the inside bottom with black suede paper.
12. Drill a small hole in the top of a plastic chess piece. Thread the tassel cord through the hole. Secure with jewelry glue. Attach tassel to handle. 👜

Painting Guide

Decoupaged Purses

The gargantuan selection of beautiful papers available can help you create all kinds of decoupaged purse designs. See the General Instructions section for information about decoupage techniques and supplies.

Mad About Mona
Cigar Box Purse

The entire front of this purse is covered with decoupage paper. You can also find this popular Leonardo da Vinci painting on calendars and museum postcards or in art books.

Supplies

Purse Base:
Ready-to-use wooden cigar box purse, 6-1/2" x 6", with bamboo handle, hinges, and latch

Decorative Materials:
Mona Lisa image cut from decoupage paper
Decoupage medium
Acrylic craft paint - Black
4" square mirror
Gold corner charm
Embossed brown suede paper (for lining)
Fine art sticker - *Mona Lisa*
Gold frame charm
Black tassel
Mat board
4" gold cord

Tools & Other Supplies:
Basecoating brush
Decoupage scissors
Craft knife
Cutting mat
Finish brush
Clear satin varnish

Instructions

1. Basecoat the box, inside and out, with black paint. Let dry.
2. Following the General Instructions for decoupage, cut and attach the paper to the front of the box.
3. Brush the box with two to three coats of satin varnish.
4. Glue the mirror and corner charm inside the lid.
5. Adhere suede paper to the inside bottom and sides.
6. Place the sticker on a piece of mat board. Cut to fit the gold frame charm.
7. Glue the mat board and gold charm together, sandwiching the gold cord hanger and the cord of the black tassel between them with the tassel hanging at the bottom.
8. Paint the back of the mat board with black acrylic paint. Let dry.
9. Attach the tassel at one side of the handle. 👜

Antique Label Purse
Cigar Box Purse

This charming design starts with a weathered and worn painted surface and has a decoupaged mix of lace and antique labels over a soft-patina surface.

Supplies

Purse Base:
Ready-to-decorate wooden cigar box purse, 6-1/2" x 6", with bamboo handle, hinges, and latch

Decorative Materials:
Acrylic craft paints - Dark green, medium green, light sage green

Peel-and-stick vintage labels

Cotton lace trim

Butterfly applique

Old linen hankie, in a matching color (for the lining)

Mat board

Polyester batting

3" round mirror

18" narrow green grosgrain ribbon (10" for the accent, 8" for the inside)

Hat charm, beads, pearls, long headed pins

Tools & Other Supplies:
Basecoating brush

Wax

Sandpaper

Water-erase marker

Fabric glue

Basecoating brush

Decoupage scissors

Craft knife

Cutting mat

Finish brush

Clear matte varnish

Instructions

1. Follow the steps for "Old Wood Decorative Finish" in the General Instructions section to paint the outside of the purse box, using all three paint colors.
2. Paint the inside with light sage green.
3. Attach vintage labels to the outside and inside lid of the box.
4. Using fabric glue, glue the lace trim and butterfly applique to the box.
5. Inside, position the mirror and trace with the marker. Using this as a guideline, attach the lace.
6. Apply two to three coats of matte varnish to the inside and outside of the purse.
7. Carefully measure and cut a piece of mat board to fit the inside bottom of the purse. Glue a piece of batting on the mat board, then cover the padded board with the hankie.
8. Position an 8" piece of green grosgrain ribbon across the padded board and glue the ends of the ribbon on the back. (The ribbon can hold business or credit cards in place on the padded bottom.)
9. Glue the padded board to the bottom of the purse.
10. String pearls and glass beads on long headed pins. Attach to a ribbon loop. Glue the gold hat charm to the ribbon to finish the tassel. Attach to one end of the handle. 👜

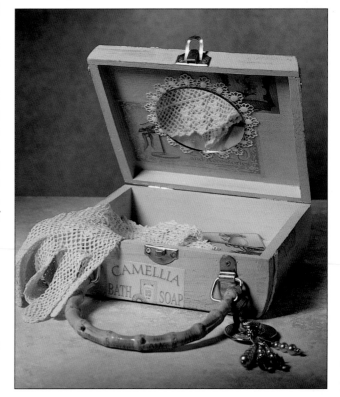

Inside of purse

Grand Adventure
Cigar Box Purse

Decoupaged motifs and rubber stamps decorate a travel-theme purse. The travel motifs came from a theme collage package. You can find collage packages at paper, crafts, and rubber stamp stores. I used alphabet stamps to add travel theme words and phrases to the design.

Supplies

Purse Base:
Ready-to-use cigar box purse, 6-1/2" x 6", with bamboo handle, hinges, and latch

Decorative Materials:
Acrylic wood stain - Oak

Paper images from traveling theme collage package

Decoupage medium

Blue permanent ink stamp pad

Rubber stamps - Postage stamp, crest, pen nib, and alphabet

3" square mirror

Brown suede paper (for lining)

Small brass handle with escutcheon

Brass key

Light brown tassel

Thin light brown cord

Tools & Other Supplies:
Basecoating brush

Craft knife

Decoupage scissors

Cutting mat

Finish brush

Clear satin varnish

Instructions

1. Stain the inside and outside of the box with oak stain. Let dry completely.
2. Cut out travel motifs and attach to the outside sides of the box. Let dry. TIP: It's okay to glue them over the seams—when dry, take a sharp craft knife and cut through the motif for a perfect match.
3. Give the entire box a topcoat of decoupage medium. Let dry.
4. Stamp images around and overlapping the paper images. TIP: To have a stamped image go around the box edge, place the stamp on the edge of the box and apply pressure to make the image. Immediately tilt the stamp over the edge and press firmly to continue the design. Let dry.
5. Coat the box with two to three coats of satin varnish.
6. Glue the mirror to the inside top of the box.
7. Line the bottom with suede paper.
8. Attach the brass handle, tassel, and key, using the photo as a guide. 👜

African Safari
Gourd Purse

This ready-to-decorate canteen gourd purse is a great example of the surfaces available to decorate and create unique purses. The shape of the gourd inspired the African safari design. I left the inside of the gourd unfinished.

Supplies

Purse Base:
Ready-to-decorate canteen gourd purse

Decorative Materials:
Printed paper napkins - African animals, animal prints
Decoupage medium, sepia-toned
Gold-tone and copper-tone varnishes
Feather tassel and beads
Animal print novelty buttons
Gold giraffe charm

Tools & Other Supplies:
Basecoating brush
Jewelry glue
Craft knife
Decoupage scissors
Cutting mat

Instructions

1. Tear motifs and pieces of animal print from the paper napkins. Brush decoupage medium on the gourd and press the paper pieces over the wet medium, covering the gourd with the motifs. (See the General Instructions for details on this technique.) Don't worry about covering the seam—let it dry completely, then cut the paper with a sharp craft knife.

2. Brush the entire surface with sepia-toned decoupage medium and let dry. The more coats you apply, the darker the finished tone will be.

3. Brush the outside with gold- and copper-toned varnishes, blending the two colors as you paint. Let dry.

4. Top the feather tassel with beads. Attach to one side of the strap.

5. Glue animal print buttons at the ends of the strap. Glue a gold giraffe charm on the front. 👜

Wine Country
Wooden Box Purse

This decoupaged box purse is covered with wine theme images and papers. It's fun to save labels from wines from memorable occasions and use them to make a very special purse.

Supplies

Base, Handle & Hardware:
Wooden box with rounded sides and hinges, 9-1/2" x 5-1/2"
Burnt bamboo handle
2 brass handle loops
2 brass handle clamps
Brass latch

Decorative Materials:
Cork decorative paper
Grape decoupage paper
Wine labels
Wine-theme paper napkins
Decoupage medium, sepia-toned
Brown suede paper (for lining)
Brown tassel

Tools:
Craft knife
Decoupage scissors
Cutting mat
Finish brush
Screwdriver & Awl

Instructions

1. Following the steps for decoupage in the General Instructions, cover the top of the box with cork decorative paper.
2. Add torn paper napkin pieces to the top and sides of the box.
3. Cut out grape motifs, wine labels and corks. Decoupage to the outside and top of the box.
4. Coat the outside and inside of the box with two coats of sepia decoupage medium. Let dry.
5. Attach the latch and handle to the box.
6. Measure and cut the suede paper. Attach to the inside top and bottom.
7. Add the tassel to the handle. 👜

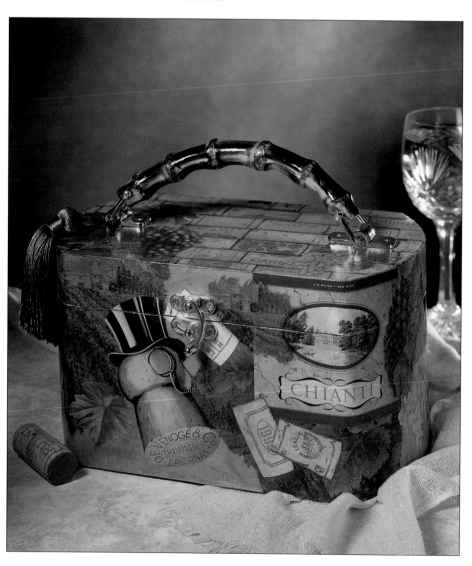

Debba's Purse
Wooden Purse Box

This decoupaged box has a black, white, and yellow color scheme. The checked bead that adorns the tassel inspired the design—I found it at a bead shop while shopping with my friend Debba. I hope she likes this purse; I named it after her!

Supplies

Base, Handles, & Hardware:
Wooden box with hinges, 4" x 8"
Black resin U-shaped handle
2 brass handle loops
2 brass handle clamps
Brass box latch
Two brass strap hooks, swivel style
Two brass chain hangers
Beaded shoulder strap - Heavy waxed linen cord, approximately 24 gold plastic beads and 60 yellow, black, and white glass beads

Decorative Materials:
Acrylic craft paint - Black
Black and white checked paper
Decoupage paper, black and white theme package
Decoupage medium
4" square mirror
Yellow plastic frog
Dimensional paint - Clear
Tiny clear glass marbles
Black and white checked bead
Black tassel

Tools & Other Supplies:
Basecoating brush
Craft knife
Decoupage scissors
Cutting mat
Finish brush
Clear matte varnish
Glue gun and clear glue sticks

Instructions

1. Basecoat the bottom of the box and the inside of the box with black paint.
2. Following the steps in the General Instructions, cover the top and sides of the box with papers.
3. Cover the inside bottom and top of the box with black checked paper.
4. Coat the box, inside and outside, with two coats of matte varnish. Let dry.
5. Thread the beads on the linen cord. Attach the ends to the strap hooks to form the beaded shoulder strap.
6. Attach the box latch, handle, and chain hangers to the box.
7. Glue the mirror to the inside lid.
8. Cover the plastic frog with the clear dimensional paint and sprinkle with the tiny glass marbles. When dry, glue inside the lid with hot glue. 👜

Nightlife
Wooden Box Purse

This sparkling cocktail purse is covered, appropriately, with cocktails! The inside reveals a mosaic of mirror squares.

Supplies

Base, Handle, & Hardware:
Wooden box with rounded ends,
4-1/4" x 7-1/2", original hinges and
latch removed
Silver bead handle frame
16-18 silver plastic beads, variety of
shapes and sizes
2 silver handle clamps
Silver latch
Silver hinges

Decorative Materials:
Cocktail theme images
Decoupage papers theme package - Cocktails
Decoupage medium, pearl-finish
Acrylic craft paint - Light lilac
5 mirrors, 1" square
10 mirrors, 1/2" square
Silver martini charm
Clear rhinestones
3" silver bead-and-sequin fringe
Silver beads
Silver cord

Tools & Other Supplies:
Basecoating brush
Jewelry glue
Craft knife
Decoupage scissors
Cutting mat
Finish brush
Screwdriver & Awl

Instructions

1. Basecoat the inside of the box and the outside bottom with lilac paint. Let dry.
2. Following the steps for decoupage in the General Instructions section, cover the top and sides of the box with decorative papers. Add decorative papers to the inside lid and bottom of the box.
3. Cut out cocktail motifs and decoupage to the outside of the box.
4. Coat all the paper and painted surfaces with two coats of the pearl decoupage medium.
5. Construct the beaded handle by threading the beads on the handle frame. Attach to the purse.
6. Attach the hinges, latch, and handle clamps to the box.
7. Create the mirror mosaic inside the lid with the square mirrors. Accent with the silver charm.
8. Make a tassel with a bead-and-sequin fringe, silver cord, and silver beads. Attach to one side of the handle.
9. Glue the rhinestones to the box with the jewelry glue. 👜

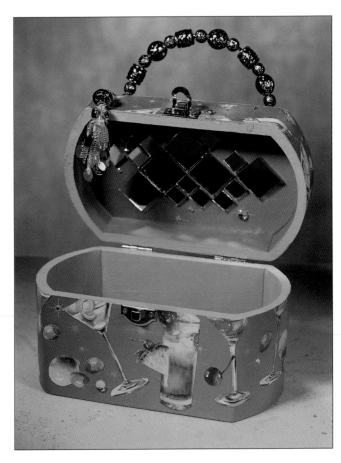

Oriental Lacquer *continued*

5. Remove any resin drips. Assemble the box with the hinges and the box latch.
6. Attach the purse handle.
7. Glue the newspaper to the inside bottom of the box.
8. Coat the inside of the box with two to three coats of satin varnish.
9. Affix the chain hangers and attach the shoulder strap.
10. Hang the tassel and carved pendant from the handle. 👝

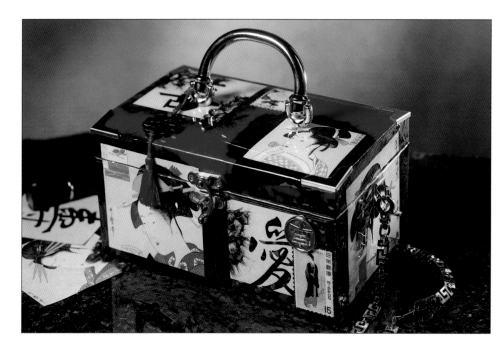

Reclining Lady
Cigar Box Purse

Beautiful prints cover both sides of this decoupaged box, and a leopard-print lining was chosen to coordinate with the leopard skin in one of the prints. The resin coating was sprayed with matte varnish for a soft, low-sheen look.

Supplies

Base, Hardware, & Handle:
Blank wooden cigar box, 8" x 12"
Burnt bamboo purse handle
2 brass handle loops
2 brass handle clamps
Brass box latch
2 brass box hinges

Decorative Materials:
Acrylic craft paint - Dark brown
Decoupage paper - Print of *The Betrothed*, leopard print
Decoupage medium
Champagne tassel accented with beads
Leopard print fabric (for lining)

Tools & Other Supplies:
White glue

Basecoating brush
Craft knife
Decoupage scissors
Cutting mat
Finish brush
Clear satin varnish
Two-part resin coating *plus* Basic Coating Supplies
Clear exterior matte spray varnish
Screwdriver & awl

Instructions

1. Paint all the surfaces of the box lid and base, inside and out, with dark brown paint.
2. Cut the images from the decoupage paper, following Chalk Transfer Method described in the Decoupage section of the General Instructions.
3. Using the decoupage medium, adhere the papers to the outside of the box.
4. Seal the images with two thin coats of white glue.
5. Following the steps in the technique section, coat the base and lid of the box with two-part resin. Let dry.
6. Spray the base and lid with matte varnish. Let dry.
7. Remove any resin drips and assemble the box with the hinges and the latch.
8. Attach the purse handle.
9. Brush the inside of the box with two to three coats of satin varnish.
10. Glue the leopard print fabric to the inside bottom and sides of the box.
11. Hang the tassel from the handle. 👝

Cigar Labels
Cigar Box Purse

This purse is meant to look like an authentic cigar box. A decoupage paper sheet of antique cigar box labels provided the images; I added lettering with matching alphabet stickers and gold seals and decorative borders. You can find these paper pieces at memory crafting, rubber stamping, and crafts stores.

Supplies

Base, Handle, & Hardware:

Blank wooden cigar box, 8" x 12"
Beaded purse handle
2 brass handle clamps
2 brass hinges
Brass box latch

Decorative Materials:

Acrylic wood stain - oak
Decoupage paper with cigar labels
Alphabet stickers
Red background decorative paper
Gold border stickers
Gold seal labels
Decoupage medium
Tiger print fabric (for lining)
Mirror with four brass corners
Cream tassel

Tools & Other Supplies:

Two-part resin coating plus Basic Coating Supplies
White glue
Basecoating brush
Craft knife
Metal ruler
Cutting mat
Screwdriver & awl
Finish Brush

Instructions

1. Stain all surfaces of the box lid and base, inside and out, with oak wood stain.
2. Cut out the label motifs from the decoupage paper. Cut the red-background paper into 1/4" strips with a craft knife.
3. Using decoupage medium, attach the papers to the outside of the box.
4. Seal all the images with two thin coats of white glue.
5. Following the steps in this section, coat the base and lid of the box with two-part resin. Let dry.
6. Remove any resin drips. Assemble the box with the hinges and latch.
7. Attach the purse handle.
8. Glue the tiger print fabric to the inside bottom and lid of the box.
9. Attach the mirror to the middle of the lid.
10. Hang the tassel from the handle. 👜

Back side of purse

Knight in Shining Armor
Cigar Box Purse

This purse has luxurious-looking gold embellishments and a beautiful sponged finish. This purse has a handle as well as a chain shoulder strap.

Supplies

Base, Hardware, & Handles:
Blank wooden cigar box, 8" x 12"
Faux tortoise shell purse handle
2 brass handle clamps
Brass box latch
2 brass box hinges
2 brass chain hangers
40" gold purse chain with strap hooks

Decorative Materials:
Acrylic craft paints - Dark plum, burgundy, light coral
Decoupage papers, romance-theme that includes one large painting-type print and some florals
Decoupage medium
White glue
Gold border stickers
4 brass metal corner charms
Oval gold metal frame, 3-1/2" x 5"
Gold tassel

Tools & Other Supplies:
Basecoating brush
Sea sponge with a fine texture
Craft knife
Metal ruler
Cutting mat
Two-part resin coating *plus* Basic Coating Supplies
Screwdriver & Awl

Instructions

1. Paint all the surfaces of the box lid and base, inside and out, with dark plum acrylic paint.
2. Sponge the outside of the lid and base, first with burgundy, then with light coral. See the General Instructions.
3. Cut motifs from the decoupage paper. Trim a large motif for the front of the purse to 7" x 10" with an art knife, ruler and cutting board. Trim another motif in an oval shape to fit the oval frame. Cut out a selection of flowers for the back.
4. Using decoupage medium, attach the print to the front of the box. Attach the oval print to the back of the box.
5. Add gold sticker borders around the large image on front.
6. Seal all the images with two thin coats of white glue.
7. Glue on the oval metal frame.
8. Glue the floral prints around the oval frame, overlapping some onto the frame.
9. Seal the floral images with two thin coats of white glue.
10. Following the steps at the beginning of this section, coat the box with two-part resin.
11. While the resin is still tacky, place the decorative corner charms around the large motif. Let dry completely.
12. Remove any resin drips.
13. Assemble the box with the hinges and the box latch. Attach the purse handle.
14. Affix the chain hangers and attach the shoulder strap.
15. Hang the tassel from the handle.
16. Finish the inside of box as you desire.

Back of purse

74

Wabi-Sabi
Cigar Box Purse

Wabi-sabi is a Japanese concept that finds beauty in things imperfect and old. The color spectrum of wabi-sabi includes earthy reds and browns, weathered blues and purples, metals and sage greens.

Supplies

Base & Hardware & Handle
Cardboard cigar box, 4-1/2" x 4-1/2" x 2-1/4"

Box latch - Gold elastic cord, Chinese coin, large purple bead

36" beaded shoulder strap - Copper, gold and ivory beads on waxed linen cord and attached to chain hooks

2 brass chain hangers

4 brass box corners

Decorative Materials:
Decorative papers - Metallic copper, washi paper, Asian collage images

Decoupage medium

Metal bamboo frame, 2" x 2"

Grosgrain ribbon (for hinge)

Mat board

Asian design fabric

Narrow tan braid trim

Gold tassel

Beads, 3-4

Carved pendant

Thin gold cord

Tools & Other Supplies:
Thin-bodied white glue

Thick white craft glue

Two-part resin coating *plus* Basic Coating Supplies

Craft knife

Cutting mat

Decoupage scissors

Metal ruler

Instructions

1. Carefully cut the lid from the base with a craft knife.
2. Cover the box base and lid with metallic copper paper, folding the excess to the inside and back.
3. Cut motifs from collage paper.
4. Using decoupage medium, attach the motifs to the outside of the box.
5. Seal all the images with two thin coats of white glue.
6. Glue the bamboo frame to the front of the box, framing a motif.
7. Following the steps at the beginning of this section, coat the base and lid of the box with two-part resin. Let dry completely.
8. Remove any resin drips.
9. Carefully measure and cut the mat board to fit inside all sides of the box.
10. Cover each piece of mat board with Asian fabric.
11. Add a piece of ribbon for the box hinge, gluing it in place with thick craft glue and attaching the lid to the box.
12. Add a 2" gold elastic loop to the top of the lid. On the top of the box base, pierce a hole and thread the large purple bead and coin to finish the latch.
13. Glue the covered mat board pieces to the insides of the box. (This hides the mechanics of the hinge and latch.)
14. Glue tan braid around the lid edge.
15. Affix the chain hangers and attach the beaded shoulder strap.
16. String the beads and carved pendant on gold cord. Add the tassel. Attach to the chain hanger. 👜

Back of purse

Casino Nights
Cigar Box Purse

I made my own decorative paper for this purse by color photocopying playing cards and poker chips and used some of the paper to line the purse. Dice were drilled and added to the beaded handle. Only the front of the purse was coated with the resin; a dam was made with decorative embellishments to prevent the resin from flowing over the sides. Be careful walking into a casino with this purse—admirers may ambush you!

Supplies

Base & Handle:
Ready-to-decorate cigar box purse, 8-1/2" x 8", with hinges and latch, original handle removed
Brass handle frame
Handle clamps
4 drilled dice
Wooden beads for handle
Gold plastic beads for handle

Decorative Materials:
Acrylic craft paint - Black
Photocopied cards and poker chips
Letter tiles - to spell "LUCK," "FORTUNE," "CHANCE," "RICH"
Faux silver and gold coins
Clear acrylic rhinestones, variety of shapes and sizes
Gold charms with casino theme
1 drilled dice
Beads
Black cord

Tools & Other Supplies:
Basecoating brush
Craft knife
Decoupage Scissors
Cutting mat
Clear satin varnish
Two-part resin coating *plus* Basic Coating Supplies
Screwdriver & Awl

Instructions

1. Paint all the surfaces of the box lid and base, inside and out, with the black acrylic paint.
2. Create the decorative paper by color photocopying a winning hand of cards and a sheet of cards and poker chips. (I used an 8-1/2" x 11" sheet of paper and glued the cards in place to create a master for copying.)
3. Cut out the hand of cards and, using decoupage medium, attach to the purse front.
4. Measure and cut some of the paper to fit the inside of the box lid.
5. Seal the front card image with two thin coats of white glue.
6. Glue the letter tiles to the front of the box at the edges. Fill in the spaces with the gold charms, faux coins and rhinestones.
7. Glue small round rhinestones to the hand of cards motif.
8. Following the steps in the beginning of this section, coat the lid of the box with two-part resin.
9. Thread the beads onto the handle frame and attach to the box top.
10. Brush the inside of the box and the un-coated outside with two to three coats of satin varnish.
11. Fashion an ornament from one drilled die, beads, and black cord. Hang from the handle. 👜

Image Transfer Purses

For the purses in this section, I found creating the image on a piece of fabric and attaching the fabric to the purse base worked best. You can buy products that enable you to easily transfer an image to fabric.

To use images and photos from your **computer**, you'll find **transfer paper** at office supply outlets that fits your printer and can be ironed on fabric. You can also buy transfer paper on which you can color photocopy motifs and then transfer the motifs to fabric. This method requires you to soak the transfer paper off the fabric after ironing. Both products give excellent results and come with detailed instructions.

Tips:

- Make sure to reverse the image when you print or photocopy it on transfer paper, **especially** if the image contains lettering.
- Choose a heavy cotton broadcloth in a light color for transferring. Cut the fabric with a rotary cutter about 1/2" larger than the original image. (This gives you room to add decorative trim.)
- Iron the image on a firm surface. A tabletop protected with towels works better than a soft, padded ironing board. Use the high (cotton) setting with no steam, and keep the iron moving to prevent scorching.

- Let cool completely before attempting to remove the paper backing to reveal the image.

After you have created the fabric image, you can attach it to the purse using one of several methods.

***Option 1:* Use fusible adhesive.**

Fusible adhesive works well on tote bags that have a smooth, flat surface. Protect the image with a piece of cooking parchment paper to avoid marring it while ironing. Follow the instructions in the section on applique for using fusible adhesive.

***Option #2.* Gluing with fabric glue.**

This method works for fabric purse blanks that cannot lie flat. The fabric image is glued at the edges with a thin line of fabric glue, and the edges are covered with trim. If the fabric piece is large, attach it in the center by sewing on decorative buttons or adding studs. Decorative pins and embroidered stitches also can be used to attach the image.

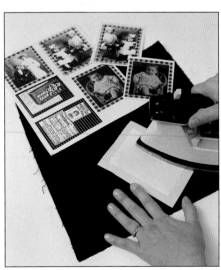

Transferring an image by ironing

Soaking the ironed transfer paper and fabric in water

Lifting off the paper to reveal the transferred image

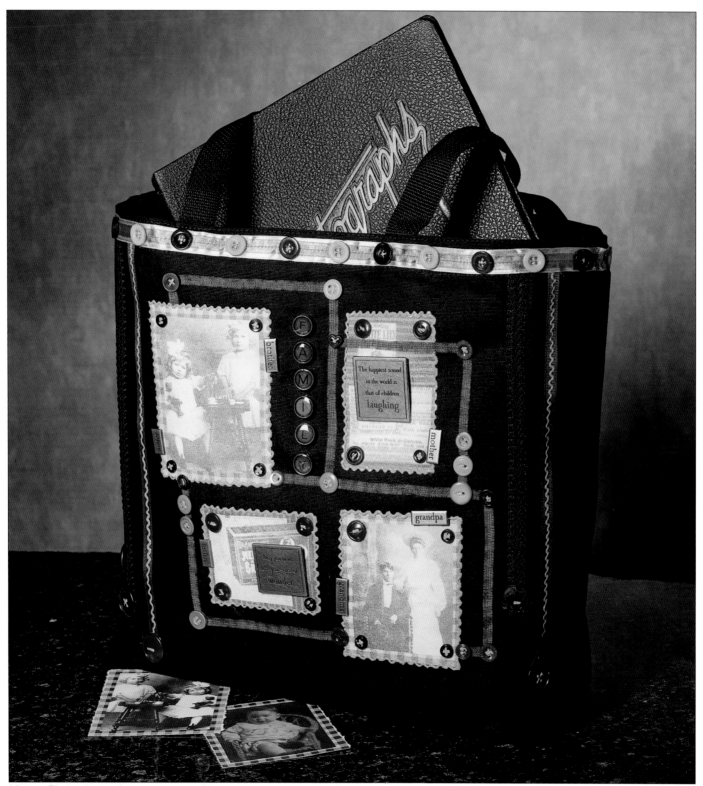

Vintage Photos. Instructions are on page 82.

Vintage Photos
Fabric Tote
Pictured on page 81.

Why pack away cherished old photos when you can display them with style on a tote bag? This bag uses memory-crafting embellishments that are readily available in stores and a black, brown, sepia, peach, and tan color theme. Decide your color theme when choosing embellishments.

Supplies

Purse Base:
Black tote bag

Decorative Materials:
Transfer paper for color photocopier
Images (old photos)
White cotton fabric for image base
Fusible adhesive
Metal key and resin alphabet charms
Selection of buttons, various sizes in matching colors
Dimensional paint - Tan
Satin ribbon trim with buttons
Variety of trims and decorative fibers in coordinating colors
Metal quote tags with family theme

Tools & Other Supplies:
Fabric glue
White paper
Eyelet setter

Instructions

1. On an 8-1/2" x 11" sheet of white paper, assemble a master sheet of photographs and images. (If you do this, you'll have less wasted transfer paper.)
2. Following the instructions at the beginning of this section, print the images and transfer them to cotton fabric panels cut 1/2" larger on all sides than the images. TIP: If there are words or letters in your photo, remember to copy it in reverse.
3. With fusible adhesive, adhere the trimmed images to the front of the tote bag.
4. With fabric glue, attach the decorative trims, buttons, and resin alphabet charms to frame and accent the photographs. Let dry completely.
5. With dimensional paint, paint borders to accent the images. Add the stitch details to the buttons. Let dry.
6. Glue the ribbon and button trim to the top edge of the tote.
7. Attach the metal quote tags, using an eyelet setter. 👜

Images of Paris
Fabric Purse
Pictured at right.

This purse is decorated with a collage made from a collage package I found in a crafts store. The images were arranged, then photocopied on transfer paper. (This allows you to make numerous copies of your master collage in any size you choose.)
Pieces of jewelry, charms, and studs provide three-dimensional accents and help secure the collage to the purse.

Supplies

Purse Base:
Canvas purse blank - natural, 11" x 10"

Decorative Materials:
Images - French collage pieces from a purchased package
Transfer paper (type for color photocopier)
Cotton fabric panel, 12" x 12"
46" dark brown grosgrain ribbon, 3/8" wide
20" cotton lace trim
4 large buttons
Pins - Rhinestone Eiffel tower, Paris
Charms - Metal key, resin alphabet
Needle and brown embroidery thread
Alphabet letter studs
Diamond-shaped mirrors
Dimensional paint - Tan
Tiny glass marbles
Black fringed tassel with beads

Tools & Other Supplies:
Fabric glue
White paper

Instructions

1. On a sheet of 10" x 10" white paper, arrange and compose your collage, layering the images and keeping the arrangement simple.

2. Following the instructions at the beginning of this section, photocopy the collage and transfer the image to the cotton fabric panel. TIP: If there are words or letters in your collage, remember to copy it in reverse.

3. With fabric glue, glue the lace trim to the top and bottom edges of the purse front.

4. Trim the transferred image to 10" x 10". Apply glue to the edges and position at the center of the purse.

5. Cut pieces of brown ribbon to frame the image and glue in place. Glue the buttons to each corner to hide the cut ends. Glue the diamond mirrors on the right side of the panel. Let dry completely.

6. Squeeze out a line of dimensional paint around each mirror and sprinkle the paint with tiny glass marbles. Using dimensional paint, add the stitch details to each button. Let dry.

7. Using the photo as a guide for placement, sew the resin alphabet charms with embroidery thread, pin the pins, and attach the stud letters by pushing the prongs to the inside of the purse and bending down to hold.

8. Attach the beaded fringe tassel at one corner.

Framed Rose
Fabric Tote

This is an easy, quick design. The plain purse, purchased in a department store, was begging for embellishment. I used a computer program to print the vintage rose motif and framed it with adhesive-backed fabric.
You may not find the same purse, so adjust the sizes to fit the purse you're using.

Supplies

Purse Base:
Plain burlap purse

Decorative Materials:
Rose image from vintage print collection
Image transfer paper for inkjet printing
White broadcloth, 6" square
Adhesive-backed fabrics - Green striped
Adhesive backed trim - Rose motif

Tools & Other Supplies:
Computer with inkjet printer
Fusible adhesive
Rotary cutter
Iron

Instructions

1. Following the instructions at the beginning of this section, print and transfer the rose image to the cotton fabric panel.
2. Trim the print to a 4" square. Using fusible adhesive, attach it to the front of the purse.
3. With a rotary cutter, trim the adhesive-backed fabric and trim to fit around the print like a frame. Adhere, following the manufacturer's instructions.
4. Cut a strip of adhesive-backed fabric 2-1/2" wide to fit from one side seam to the other. Adhere along the bottom of the purse. 🔒

Daisy-Kitty
Fabric Tote

This charming, cheery tote is decorated with a favorite photograph and silk flowers. Depending on your photograph, use either color photocopy transfer paper or (for a digital photograph) inkjet printer transfer paper.

Supplies

Purse Base:
Medium denim tote bag

Decorative Materials:
Photograph of your choice
Transfer paper
Cotton fabric
8 silk daisies, 2" diameter
8 yellow buttons, 1/2" diameter
Bee charm
30" yellow rick-rack trim

Tools & Other Supplies:
Fusible adhesive
Fabric glue

Instructions

1. Following the instructions at the beginning of this section, print the photograph and transfer to a cotton fabric panel cut 1/2" larger than the image. TIP: If there are words or letters in your photo, remember to copy it in reverse.
2. Adhere the image to the front of the tote bag with fusible adhesive.
3. Remove the plastic parts from the silk daisies and leaves. Arrange the leaves and the blossoms to accent the photograph and attach with fabric glue.
4. Glue a yellow button at the center of each blossom.
5. Glue the bee charm in place.
5. Glue on yellow rick-rack to top of purse. 🔒

Appliqued Purses

Appliques are a quick and easy way to add a decorative touch to a purse. Ready-to-use beaded appliques have an adhesive backing that you simply peel off and place. You can re-position the applique at first, but after a few days it will adhere permanently. Fabric, lace, and embroidered appliques can be sewn on or attached with fabric glue. Embroidered appliques also come with an iron-on adhesive backing.

Steps for Attaching Appliques

I used wool felt appliques that I attached with fusible adhesive and accented with stitches made with dimensional paint. If you can't find wool felt, substitute craft felt.

1. Trace the applique motif on a piece of paper, creating a template.
2. Cut a piece of fusible adhesive a bit larger than the motif. Lightly fuse the adhesive to a piece of wool felt, using a dry iron set on high and following the manufacturer's instructions. Let cool.
3. Using the paper template, lightly trace the pattern outline on the paper backing of the fusible adhesive.
4. Cut out the motif with sharp scissors.
5. Peel off the backing paper. Fuse the wool felt motif to the front of a tote bag, using the hot iron. (photo 1) TIP: Don't over-iron—the adhesive qualities can be lost.
6. Repeat to adhere other appliques.
7. Use dimensional paint to add stitch marks or outlines. (photo 2) Let dry completely before using. TIP: Start in the top corner opposite your drawing hand to prevent smudging the wet paint as you work.

Photo 1. Ironing on a felt applique

Photo 2. Outlining and adding details with dimensional paint

Autumn Leaves ▶
Instructions are on page 88.

Ladybugs for Luck
Fabric Purse

This simple, cute-as-a-bug design has a faux beaded ladybug and embroidered ladybug appliques. The colorful rows of rick-rack trim and beaded handles make this a perfect casual bag for the young or young at heart.

Supplies

Base & Handle:
Small denim tote bag (converted to a handbag)
4 D-rings
20" 19-gauge black crafting wire
10 gold plastic beads
30 red, green, and black glass beads
Magnetic closure snap
Four heavy duty snaps

Decorative Materials:
2 embroidered iron-on ladybug appliques
Dimensional paint - Black, red, green
Tiny clear glass marbles
24" red rick-rack
24" green rick-rack

Tools & Other Supplies:
Iron
Fabric glue
Supplies & tools for converting a tote (see the following pages)

Instructions

1. Convert the tote bag into a purse following the instructions for "Converting a Tote Bag to Make a Purse" in the *General Instructions* section.
2. Cut two 10" pieces of wire and thread on the beads. Loop the ends around the D-rings and attach to the purse loops.
3. Transfer the ladybug pattern to the front of the purse.
4. Working one area at a time, paint the ladybug with dimensional paint and sprinkle with tiny marbles to create the beaded ladybug. Let dry completely.
5. Iron on the two embroidered appliques.
6. Attach the rick-rack with fabric glue.

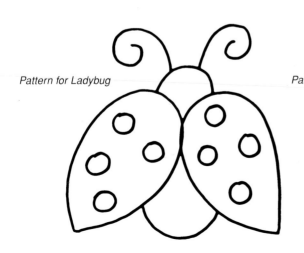
Pattern for Ladybug

Painting Guide for Ladybug

Wild Flowers
Fabric Purse

There are wonderful adhesive-backed beaded appliques available for purse designing—you simply peel off the backing and place them on the purse. They provide a quick and easy project to do with young children.

Supplies

Base & Handles:
Pink twill purse blank with button handle loops
2 clear plastic U-shaped handles

Decorative Materials:
Beaded appliques - 7 flowers, 5 swirls, floral border, dotted scalloped border
Dimensional paint - Yellow
Tiny clear glass marbles
Large green button
Pink embroidery thread
1 mm clear beading cord

Instructions

1. Apply flower and swirl appliques to the purse, using the photo as a guide. Reserve two flower appliques for the tassel.
2. Apply the borders to the clear handles and the closure flap, using the photo as a guide.
3. Make a tassel with clear beading cord. Decorate with two beaded applique flowers placed back to back with the tassel in between. Make sure you leave a loop of cord exposed at top of tassel.
4. Accent the green button with dimensional paint and tiny marbles. Make sure the buttonholes are left open. Attach to the purse with pink embroidery thread.
5. Place the tassel loop over one of the handle loops.
6. Attach handles. 👜

Colorful Buttons
Wooden Box Purse
Pattern for handle appears on page 96

Buttons in bold, colorful hues cover the front of this box purse. This is not what you normally think of as an appliqué — but most anything applied to the purse can be an appliqué. The handle is easily made from armature wire, so it's an economical and fun project for young crafters.

Supplies

Base & Handle:
6" hexagon wooden box with hinges and latch
16" of 1/8" soft aluminum armature wire
4 small screws

Decorative Materials:
Acrylic craft paint - Bright yellow
Colorful plain and novelty buttons (Reserve 16 buttons for the feet and three for the tassel.)
Blue tassel
12" of 20 gauge colored wire
Silver beads
Colorful glass beads

Tools & Other Supplies:
Jewelry glue
Gloss acrylic varnish
Paint brush
Hammer
Awl
Glue gun and glue stick

Instructions

1. Basecoat the inside and outside of the box with the yellow acrylic paint. Let dry.
2. Using the photo as a guide, glue buttons to cover the front of the purse, using jewelry glue. Let dry.
3. Glue stacks of four buttons to the bottom corners of the purse for the feet.
4. To construct the handle, coil and bend the wire using the pattern provided as a guide.
5. Using a hammer on a hard surface, flatten two 1" lengths of the wire as shown on the pattern. Create two holes on each flattened piece with an awl. With small screws, attach the handle to the box base.
6. Fold the 12" of 20 gauge wire in half. Thread the wire ends through the holes in the buttons and the beads, alternating silver beads with glass beads and buttons as shown to create a decoration 3" long. Attach the wire ends to the handles and wrap to secure.
7. With a glue gun, glue the blue tassel to the bottom of the first button. 👜

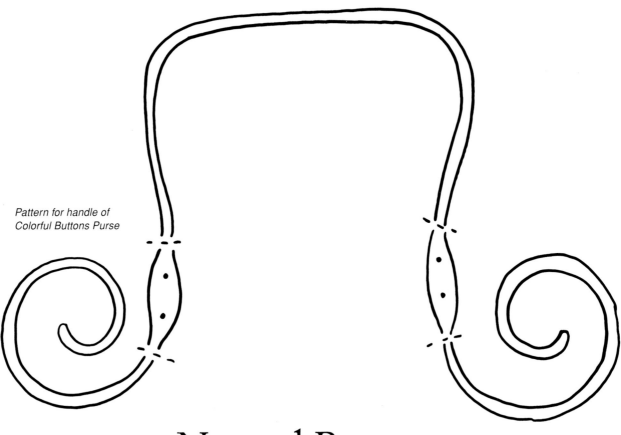

Pattern for handle of Colorful Buttons Purse

Natural Buttons
Fabric Purse
Pictured at right

A variety of buttons in similar tones give a relaxed, refined look. You could sew each button, but the purse's heavy fabric makes this difficult. Instead, use strong fabric glue to attach the buttons for a quick and easy design.

Supplies
Base & Handles:
Natural twill purse blank with button
   handle loops
4 brass handle loops
2 natural resin handles

Decorative Materials:
100 natural colored buttons, variety of
   sizes

Tools & Other Supplies:
Fabric glue
Water-erase marker
Ruler

Instructions
1. Using the marker and a ruler, mark a straight line 2-1/2" from the top of the purse.
2. Using fabric glue, attach buttons to one side of the purse. Let dry.
3. Glue buttons on the other side. Let dry.
4. Remove any marks that show with a clean sponge and water.
5. Add a large button to the closure flap.
6. Construct and attach the handles.

Ribbon Rose Purses

Ribbon roses are easy to make and add a soft, romantic touch to your purse design. (If you don't want to make ribbon roses, you can buy small satin ribbon roses in the wedding department of fabrics and crafts stores.)

Supplies for a Ribbon Rose

Wire-edge ribbon

Needle and thread (Choose a thread color that matches your ribbon; for increased visibility, black thread was used for the how-to photos.)

Flower stamen (You need 5 to 10 per flower, depending on the size of the flower center you desire.)

Basic Instructions for Ribbon Roses

1. Fold one end of the ribbon at right angles. Fold the flower stamen in half.
2. Using the needle and thread, stitch the stamen in place at the end of the ribbon at the fold. Leave the needle and thread on for the rest of the rose formation. (photo 1)
3. From the other side of the ribbon, pull the bottom wire gently to gather (ruche) the ribbon. TIP: If you pull too hard, you risk breaking the wire. (photo 2)
4. Starting at the flower center end, coil the ribbon to form the rose. (photo 3)
5. To secure, tack the layers of ribbon at the back, using a needle and thread. (photo 4)

How Much Ribbon?

For larger roses, use wider ribbon and a longer length. For smaller roses, use narrower ribbon and a shorter length. A basic formula is 2 x ribbon width (RW) x 20. For example, for ribbon 1/2" wide, you need 10"; for ribbon 1-1/2" wide, you need 30". As for size, 28" of ribbon 1-3/8" wide makes a rose 3-1/2" in diameter.

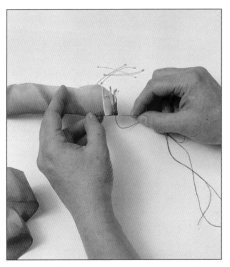

Photo 1. Making the flower center by folding down the edge around stamen

Photo 2. Pulling the wire to gather the edge of the ribbon

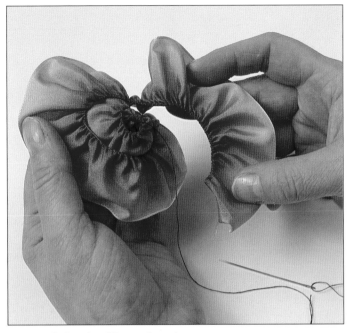

Photo 3. Coiling the ribbon to form the rose

Photo 4. Stitching at the back to secure

Golden Roses
Silk Purse
Pictured on page 100

A purchased silk pouch purse is accented with lace gold trim, pearls, and a gold ribbon rose for a rich, stylish look. All the trims and accents are sewn on with small stitches. If you wish to sew your own pouch purse, use one of the many patterns available.

Supplies

Purse Base:
Green silk purse with foldover top and a cream cord shoulder strap

Decorative Materials:
15" gold trim, 1/2" wide
55" ivory fused beads
30" gold wire-edge ribbon, 1-3/8" wide
Cream and gold flower stamen
Velvet leaves and buds
Cream tassel
Cream lace applique

Tools & Other Supplies:
Needle and matching thread

Instructions

1. Starting at the top corner, stitch the gold trim around the flap.
2. Again starting at the top edge, stitch the fused pearls around the flap. When you get to the opposite corner, wrap the pearls around the cord shoulder strap and back to where you started. Stitch the end of the pearls at the end of the cream cord to secure.
3. Stitch the lace applique in place at the bottom of the flap.
4. Stitch the velvet leaf and bud sprig to the middle of the bottom of the flap.
5. Make a ribbon rose with the gold ribbon and stamen, following the instructions at the beginning of this section. Stitch in place over the leaf stem.
6. Sew a cream tassel to the bottom of the purse. 👜

Cream Lace & Roses
Evening Bag

The lace trims, ribbon roses, and beads were hand sewn for a beautiful finish that's worthy of an heirloom. The satin rose trim can be found in the bridal departments of crafts and fabrics stores. You'll need to use very small stitches and a fine needle that can fit through the holes of the seed beads.

Supplies

Base & Handle:
Cream satin purse, 6" x 6", with magnetic closure; original handle removed
28" pearl beaded shoulder strap with silver strap hooks

Decorative Materials:
14" cream satin ribbon rose trim
Mother of pearl rice beads
Mother of pearl carved flower and leaf buttons
Ivory seed beads
Sheer ribbon flowers
12" cream lace trim, 1-1/4" wide
12" cream lace trim, 1-3/4" wide
12" cream lace and netting trim, 4-1/2" wide

Tools & Other Supplies:
Beading needle and matching thread

Instructions

1. Attach the wide lace with the edge along the bottom of the purse, placing the seam at the back.
2. Attach the 1-3/4" lace at the top of the wide lace, placing the seam at the back.
3. Attach the remaining lace around the purse top, placing the seam at the back.
4. Tack the ribbon rose trim along the top.
5. Sew the rose and bead arrangement in a cluster at the top center of the wide lace. Stitch three ribbon roses cut from the trim. Add the carved leaf and large flower buttons next.
6. Stitch the sheer ribbon flowers and the smaller flower and leaf beads.
7. To finish the cluster, add rice beads and small seed beads.
8. Attach the shoulder strap to the fabric loops. 👜

Satin & Roses
Evening Bag

A plain satin bag is made exceptional with the addition of a ribbon rose. This rose is flattened and stitched to the purse for a distinctive look. You can make a tassel to use as a zipper pull or use a purchased tassel.

Supplies

Purse Base:
Ecru satin purse, 6" x 6", with zipper top and shoulder strap

Decorative Materials:
40" peach-to-tan shaded wire-edge ribbon, 1-3/8" wide
3 velvet leaves
Gold flower stamen
12" gold beaded fringe
12" ivory braid
16" gold wire-edge ribbon, 3/8" wide
Beaded fringed tassel topped with a bead (Made with 3" of beaded fringe, a piece of braid, and a glass bead—see "How to Make Tassels.")

Tools & Other Supplies:
Needle and matching thread
Fabric glue

Instructions

1. Following the preceding Basic Instructions, construct a ribbon rose with 30" of the peach-to-tan ribbon and the stamen, pulling the wire along the dark brown edge to create a peach rose.
2. With the remaining 10" of ribbon, make a smaller ribbon rose for a bud, pulling the wire on the peach edge to create a dark brown rosebud.
3. Flatten the rose and the flower bud, shaping the wire edges. Using the needle and thread, make small stitches to hold the rose forms.
4. Glue the roses on the purse front with fabric glue.
5. Tuck two velvet leaves under the large rose and over the front of the bud. Glue in place with fabric glue and let dry.
6. Make a bow with gold ribbon. Glue in place under the ribbon roses. Let dry.
7. Glue the gold beaded fringe and braid along the top of the purse.
8. Attach the tassel to the zipper to act as a pull. 👜

Black & White Roses
Fabric Purse

I love this bright ribbon rose purse. Instead of a romantic feel, the bright colors and black and white trim combine for a contemporary, tropical look.

Supplies

Base & Handle:
Black twill purse blank with button-up handle loops
Wooden handles

Decorative Materials:
18" black and white polka wire-edge ribbon, 1-3/8" wide
30" each pink, yellow, and purple shaded wire-edge ribbon, 1-3/8" wide
Pink and yellow flower stamen
4 velvet leaves
6" black and white cord trim
Acrylic craft paint - Black

Tools & Other Supplies:
Basecoating brush
Clear gloss varnish
Needle and matching thread
Glue gun and clear glue stick

Instructions

1. Paint the handles with black paint.
2. Brush handles with two to three coats of gloss varnish. Set aside to dry.
3. Make ribbon roses with the pink, yellow, and purple ribbon and stamen, following the Basic Instructions at the beginning of this section. Set aside.
4. Using a needle and thread, sew the black and white trim to the top of the bag.
5. Sew a piece of the black and white ribbon with the raw edges folded under in position under the first trim, making small stitches all around the ribbon edge.
6. Fold one end of a 12" piece of black and white ribbon and pull the wire from the other end to gather. Gather to fit along the front of the purse, 1" down from the first piece of ribbon. Tuck the raw edges under and stitch the gathered ribbon in place.
7. With the glue gun, adhere the three roses in place. Tuck in and glue the leaves.
8. Attach the black handles. 👜

Silk Flower Purses

Silk flowers can easily dress up a plain purse. Simply remove all the plastic parts from the flower heads and leaves and glue the fabric flower pieces with a glue gun or fabric glue. You also can attach the blossoms with studs for a decorative center. At some stores, it's possible to purchase just the flower heads or petals rather than entire flowers.

Silk Petal Hydrangeas
Fabric Purse

Silk blossoms are taken off the stem and re-assembled on the front of the purse for a dazzling embellishment.

Supplies

Base & Handles:
Natural fabric purse blank with button-
   up handle loops
Wooden handles

Decorative Materials:
Silk hydrangea blossoms
Silver studs, variety of sizes
6" beaded fringe, blue and lilac hues
Acrylic craft paints - Light blue, medium
   blue

Tools & Other Supplies:
Fabric glue
Clear gloss varnish
Dense sponge
Water-erase marker
Scissors *or* stud setter

Instructions

1. Using a water-erase marker, sketch the placement of the main flower head and leaves. (You'll use this as a guide when placing the blossoms and leaves.)
2. Remove the plastic parts from the blossoms and leaves.
3. Starting with the petals from the center of the flower head, attach the blossoms with the silver studs, pushing the prongs through to the inside of the purse and bending down the prongs with a hard metal object, such as scissor handles. TIP: A stud setter makes this job much easier.
4. When the flower head is complete, glue the leaves in place with fabric glue. Let dry completely.
5. Attach the beaded fringe with a variety of silver studs, starting in the center and working towards the ends. Glue the raw fringe ends to the back of the purse side with the fabric glue.
6. Basecoat the wooden handles with light blue. Let dry.
7. Using a barely damp sponge and very little medium blue paint, shade the bottom of the handles. Let dry.
8. Apply two to three coats gloss varnish. Let dry.
9. Attach the handles. 👜

Daisy a Day
Back Pack

This whimsical backpack has brightly painted patches and is scattered with little daisies that have bright yellow button centers.

Supplies

Purse Base:
Small back pack, natural

Decorative Materials:
Acrylic craft paints - Lime green, deep lilac, bright blue
Textile medium
12 small silk daisies, 1" diameter
1 silk daisy, 2-1/2" diameter
10 yellow buttons, 1/4" diameter
8 bright yellow buttons, 1/2" diameter
24" lime green rick-rack trim
12 novelty and flower buttons - Purple, yellow, lime green, blue

Tools & Other Supplies:
Water-erase marker
Paint brush
Fabric glue

Instructions

1. With the marker, draw irregular squares on the front of the backpack. TIP: Remember the design is intentionally whimsical.
2. Mix each acrylic paint color with an equal amount of textile medium. Paint the squares with the colors. Let dry.
3. Attach rick-rack to the bottom edge of the pack and around the flap edge with fabric glue.
4. Remove the plastic parts on the small daisy blossoms. Use fabric glue to glue the daisies to the front of the pack, scattering them around and on the painted patches. For variety, give some flowers two petal layers, others just one.
5. Glue a button at the center of each blossom.
6. Remove the plastic parts on the larger daisy. Glue on the middle of the flap. Add a button center.
7. Glue the colored novelty buttons on the rick-rack edging the flap. 👜

Floral Initial
Fabric Purse

Silk flowers also can be glued on a purse in the shape of a letter to create a monogram.
This minimal design offers a cheerful floral touch. See "Making Your Own Monogram"
for instructions on how to create a computer-generated letter.

Supplies

Base & Handle:
Khaki twill purse blank with button up
   handle loops
Wooden handle with wooden beads

Decorative Materials:
24 glass beads, lilac and purple hues

22 gauge wire
Small silk flower pick with lilac blossoms
24" lavender rick-rack
1 natural-colored button

Tools & Other Supplies:
Fabric glue
Computer-generated letter
Water-erase transfer paper
Wire cutters
Pliers

Instructions

1. Glue the rick-rack around the rim of the purse.
2. Stitch the button to the front of the flap.
3. Transfer the letter to the front of the purse on the right side.
4. Cut the stems off the flowers so they will fit flat on the surface.
5. Use the transferred letter as a guide for gluing on the blossoms with the fabric glue, adding leaves as well as the little buds to create the design. Create a variety of thick and thin lines, from a thin line of buds to a thicker arrangement with the blossom heads. Leave the purse flat until the glue is completely dry.
6. Cut apart the original wooden bead handle and replace some of the wooden beads with glass beads to match the flower colors. 👜

Purple Rose
Denim Fabric Purse

You can find containers of silk flower petals in the bridal departments of some crafts and fabrics stores. You can use them to create this giant rose on the front of a purse. What fun you will have with this bag.

Supplies

Base & Handles:
Small denim tote bag converted to a handbag
Wooden handles

Decorative Materials:
Lilac sheer silk rose petals
Pink button
Pink and white flower stamen
Acrylic craft paint - Light purple

Tools & Other Supplies:
Water-erase marker
Basecoating brush
Clear gloss varnish
Glue gun and clear glue sticks
Protractor

Instructions

1. Using the instructions for "Converting a Tote Bag to Make a Purse" in the Appliqued Purses section, convert the denim tote bag into a purse.
2. Using a protractor, draw a circle 8" diameter in the middle of the purse front.
3. Use the circle as a guide, glue the rose petals on the purse, starting from the outside in, overlapping the rows as you work towards the center. When you get to the center, trim five petals (to make them smaller) and glue to form the center of the rose.
4. Glue the stamen around the back of the button. Glue the button at the center of the rose.
5. Paint the wooden handles with light purple paint. Let dry.
6. Finish the handles with two to three coats of gloss varnish. Let dry.
7. Attach handles to bag. 👜

No-Sew
Placemat Purses

This technique uses a placemat to make an attractive, practical purse. The beauty of a placemat is that it comes lined, with all the sides finished. I used standard-sized placemats, 13" x 19-1/2"—some were a touch larger or smaller, but wooden pieces of the same size worked fine for all of them.
If you like, you could easily substitute a heavy fabric or a lined piece of cotton fabric for the mat.

Basic Supplies for a Placemat Purse

Placemat, 13" x 19-1/2"
Water-erase marker
Ruler
2 pieces 3/4" pine, each 6" x 2-1/2"
Acrylic craft paint to match the placemat
Varnish
Handles with handle loops
Heavy mat board, 2-1/2" x 12"
Small hammer
Finishing nails, 1/2" long (You also can use a staple gun.)
3 yds. trim, such as grosgrain or satin ribbon or braid
Fabric glue
Sandpaper
Optional: Decorative wood pieces for the sides, 2 chain hangers and shoulder strap with strap hooks, glue gun and glue sticks

Basic Instructions

1. To prepare the wood pieces, sand all the edges smooth.
2. *Option:* Add decorative wooden pieces to the sides.
3. Paint all sides of the wood pieces to match your place mat. Let dry.
4. Varnish the painted wood pieces with two to three coats. Let dry.
5. Measure and mark the center of the bottom of the outside edges of the wood pieces. Measure and mark the inside center of the mat along the long sides. (photo 1)
6. Line up the marks and nail the sides of the placemat to the wood, pulling the mat taut and placing nails 1" apart. Repeat on the other side. (photo 2)
7. Place the mat board in the bottom of the bag to hold the shape. Make sure you have a good fit—depending on the size of your placemat, you may need a smaller or larger piece. *Option:* Glue the mat board to the placemat with a glue gun.
8. Starting at the bottom of the purse, under the wood piece, glue trim around the edge of the placemat up and around the inside of the mat and along the top of the wood piece. Repeat on the other side. (photo 3)
9. Mark the placement for the handles. Loop the trim through a handle loop and glue to hold. Glue the trim around the purse to the other side and loop through the other handle. Repeat on the other side. (photo 4) TIP: Use a glue gun to make an immediate bond.
10. *Option:* Attach the chain hangers to the decorative wood pieces. Attach the shoulder strap. 👜

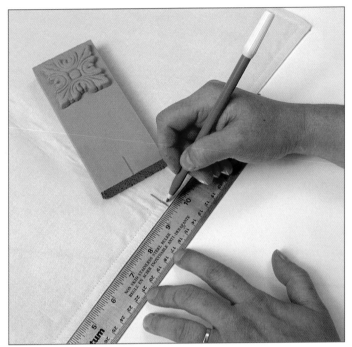

Photo 1. Measuring and marking the center of the placemat and wood pieces

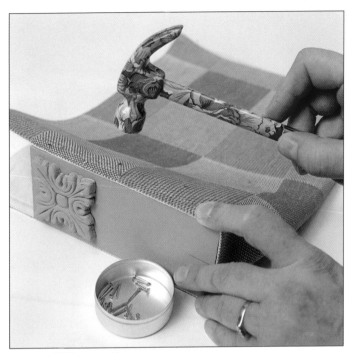

Photo 2. Nailing the sides

Photo 3. Gluing the decorative trim over the nails

Photo 4. Adding handles with strips of trim

Bamboo Mat
Fabric Purse
Pictured Opposite

*For this purse, I left the wooden sides their natural
wood color and varnished them.*

Supplies

Base & Handles:
Bamboo placemat
2 pieces of 3/4" pine for sides, 6" x 2-1/2"
Bamboo handles with brass handle loops

Decorative Materials:
3 yds. ecru grosgrain ribbon, 1" wide

Tools & Other Supplies:
Varnish
Varnish brush
Basic Supplies for a Placemat Purse

Instructions

1. Varnish the wood pieces. Let dry.
2. Assemble the purse, following the steps in the Basic Instructions for this section. 👜

Floral Mats
Fabric Purse
Pictured on page 118.

Supplies

Base & Handles:
Floral print placemat
2 pieces of 3/4" pine for sides, 6 x 2-1/2"
Bamboo handles, two 6" lengths

Decorative Materials:
1-1/2 yds. moss green satin ribbon, 1/4 " wide
1-1/2 yds. moss green satin ribbon, 5/8" wide
Acrylic craft paint - ivory
Matte varnish

Tools & Other Supplies:
Basic Supplies for a Placemat Purse
Paint brushes

Instructions

1. Paint the wood pieces with ivory paint. Let dry.
2. Varnish wood pieces with matte varnish. Let dry.
3. Assemble the purse, following the steps in the Basic Instructions for this section. 👜

Taupe Squares
Fabric Purse

Supplies

Base & Handles:
Taupe and tan square patterned placemat
2 pieces of 3/4" pine for sides, 6 x 2-1/2
Rope handles with wooden handle loops
2 brass chain hangers
Leather strap with brass swivel strap
  hooks

Decorative Materials:
3 yds. natural braided ribbon, 3/4 " wide
2 decorative wood pieces
Acrylic craft paint - Light tan
Matte varnish

Tools & Other Supplies:
Basic Supplies for a Placemat Purse
Paint brushes
Wood glue

Instructions

1. Paint the wooden side pieces and the decorative wood trim pieces with light tan paint. Let dry.
2. Varnish wood pieces with matte varnish. Let dry.
3. Glue the decorative wood pieces to the side pieces.
4. Assemble the purse, following the steps in the Basic Instructions for this section. 👜

◄ *Floral Mats*
Instructions appear on page 116.

Gallery of Purses

This section includes designs from designers around North America to inspire you.

Patricia Landry and Linda Michaluk
British Columbia, Canada
www.swallowhillcreations.com

Patricia and Linda create lovely beaded crocheted and knitted bags and a line of gorgeous scarves. Their company, Swallow Hill Creations, also offers make-it-yourself kits

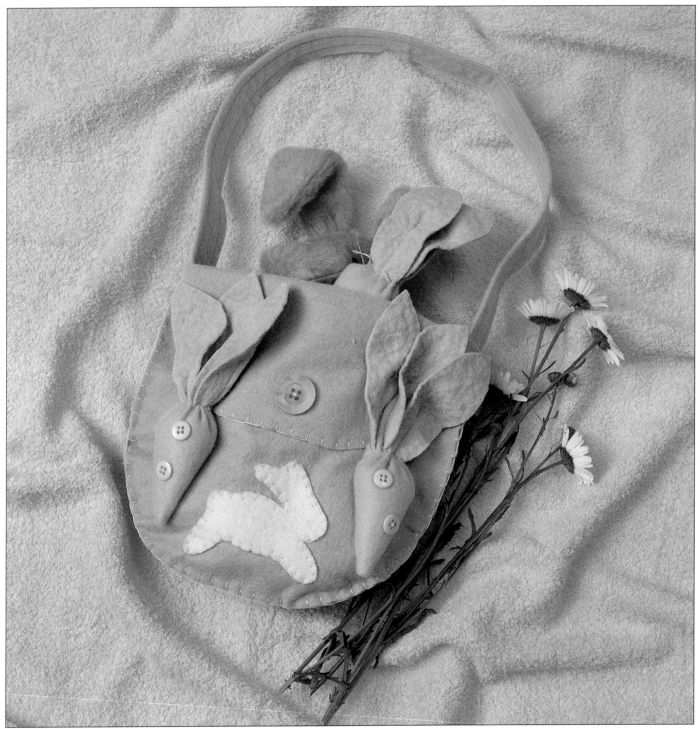

Debra Quartermain
New Brunswick, Canada
www.homespuntreasuresdesigns.com

This whimsical wool felt purse can hold a little girl's treasures as well as an adorable, playful bunny. Blanket-stitched details and dainty buttons add to the charm.

Debra is a designer and author in the craft industry who works with magazine editors, manufacturers, and publishers.

Cindy Gorder
Wisconsin, USA

Cindy is a career graphic designer who enjoys crafting in many mediums. For this purse, she scanned clip art, manipulated it, and printed it on various papers. Then she cut out and assembled this charming purse stationery set, complete with hankie notes.

Debba Haubert
Cincinnati, Ohio, USA
www.bobella.com

Debba provides marketing, product development, sales support and design for the craft and hobby industry. Her designs have been published in numerous magazines and books.

Holes are drilled in a plastic box to wire together and attach drilled dice feet, latch and beaded handle. Clip art decal creates stickers for the purse sides.

Sharon M. Reinhart, SCD, CPD, CCD
Alberta, Canada

Sharon embellished a purse she bought in a department store with leather pieces, lacing, faux leather fringe, polymer clay, rubber stamping, nylon window screen, and star nail-heads.

A designer, author, teacher, and demonstrator, Sharon is a Certified Professional Demonstrator, Certified Craft Designer, and a member of the Society of Craft Designers and The Hobby Industry Association.

*Elaine Jackson
Nevada, USA
www.birdandflower.com*

Elaine is a joyful creator whose work amazes and inspires people. These purses are made from a pattern designed by Amy Butler; the fabric was created by block printing on drapery blackout fabric. The purses have a crackle finish and decorative stitching around the edges.

Gail Kushner
Arizona, USA

Gail is a craft designer whose work appears in national magazines and books. Her clear purse box design was decorated with her signature "wild girl" motif, made with plastic, beads, and curled wire hair. Sequin trim, beads, and feathers adorn this fun, displayable design.

Metric Conversion Chart

Inches to Millimeters and Centimeters

Inches	MM	CM	Inches	MM	CM
1/8	3	.3	2	51	5.1
1/4	6	.6	3	76	7.6
3/8	10	1.0	4	102	10.2
1/2	13	1.3	5	127	12.7
5/8	16	1.6	6	152	15.2
3/4	19	1.9	7	178	17.8
7/8	22	2.2	8	203	20.3
1	25	2.5	9	229	22.9
1-1/4	32	3.2	10	254	25.4
1-1/2	38	3.8	11	279	27.9
1-3/4	44	4.4	12	305	30.5

Yards to Meters

Yards	Meters	Yards	Meters
1/8	.11	3	2.74
1/4	.23	4	3.66
3/8	.34	5	4.57
1/2	.46	6	5.49
5/8	.57	7	6.40
3/4	.69	8	7.32
7/8	.80	9	8.23
1	.91	10	9.14
2	1.83		

Index